Raising a Behaviorally Healthy Puppy

A PET PARENTING GUIDE

by Suzanne Hetts, Ph.D.
and Daniel Q. Estep, Ph.D.
Certified Applied Animal Behaviorists

ISBN 0-97495424-1

Library of Congress Control Number: 2004096634

Island Dog Press, Inc.
4994 S. Independence Way
Littleton, Colorado 80123

Dedication

This book is dedicated to our Irish Setter puppy, Firefly's Coral Lady, who has reminded us what it's like to be puppy parents. Coral brought us laughter, love, and interrupted sleep, taught us patience, and helped us expand our creative problem ability. And the best gift of all–puppy breath.

Table of Contents

Acknowledgments

We would like to thank a number of people who helped make this book possible. Thanks to Dr. Stephen Zawistowski of the American Society for the Prevention of Cruelty to Animals. We owe a great debt of gratitude to our graphic artist and book designer, Kristi Endelicato of Metagraphics for bearing with all our changes and producing a great looking book.

Special thanks to the participants in our workshop, "Implementing Puppy Classes in the Veterinary Clinic," and to all the veterinarians, staff and puppy owners who have given us feedback on earlier versions of this book.

Our sincere and heartfelt thanks to Marsha Heinke, DVM, EA, CPA and Larry Forthofer, DVM, a powerhouse husband and wife veterinary team, for their contribution of Chapter 2 on wellness care for puppies. We are lucky to have Marsha and Larry not only as colleagues, but personal friends, who share our commitment to helping people create quality relationships with their animal companions. Dr. Heinke and Dr. Forthofer own Forever Friends Pet Care Center, a premier pet resort with lodging, hydrotherapy and training services, and Forever Friends Pet Hospital in Grafton OH. Dr. Heinke is also a certified veterinary practice manager, whose firm provides services to support the successful operation of veterinary practices.

ABOUT THE AUTHORS

Suzanne Hetts, Ph.D. Applied Animal Behaviorist

Suzanne Hetts holds a doctorate in animal behavior from Colorado State University. She is certified by the Animal Behavior Society as an applied animal behaviorist.

Dr. Hetts has helped thousands of pet parents to improve their pets' behavior and relationships. She is often called upon to consult with animal professionals, veterinarians, dog trainers, humane societies and personal injury attorneys to help them understand and work with animal issues.

Dr. Hetts is a popular, award-winning, international speaker, and author of *Pet Behavior Protocols: What to Say, What to Do, When to Refer*, published by AAHA Press and coauthor of *Help! I'm Barking and I Can't Be Quiet: A Pet Parenting Guide*, published by Island Dog Press, Inc. She directed the Delta Society's *Professional Standards for Dog Trainers* project and consults with major corporations in the pet industry. Her publications and videos are used in nationwide training programs for animal caretakers and pet parents.

Daniel Q. Estep, Ph.D. Applied Animal Behaviorist

Daniel Q. Estep holds a doctorate in psychology with a specialization in animal behavior from the University of Florida. He is certified by the Animal Behavior Society as an applied animal behaviorist.

Dr. Estep is internationally respected as a teacher, researcher, and lecturer in animal behavior. He regularly consults with veterinarians, pet professionals, humane organizations, government agencies and attorneys about animal behavior. He has published a variety of research papers and books as well as numerous articles for pet owners. He is coauthor of *Help I'm Barking and I Can't Be Quiet: A Pet Parenting Guide* and numerous video and audio training programs for pet professionals and pet parents.

Drs. Hetts and Estep own Animal Behavior Associates, Inc., a pet behavior consulting firm in Littleton, Colorado. Their firm provides professional animal consulting services to organizations and pet owners throughout North America and the world. They maintain a popular and active Web site (www.AnimalBehaviorAssociates.com) which contains a wealth of information for pet parents and pet professionals. They share their home and their lives with Buffett the cat, Dalmatian Ashley and Irish Setter Coral.

Chapter 1
Wellness Care for Your Puppy's Behavioral Health

Congratulations on adding a new puppy to your family! You are starting on a journey that should last until your puppy becomes a gray-faced senior. Despite the unavoidable bumps along the way, those years should be filled with fun and love as you and your dog share each other's lives. Puppyhood is crucially important to you and your puppy. It's both an incredibly fun time and a tremendous responsibility.

There is no other time you can have more influence over your puppy's behavior and the type of dog she becomes than now. You won't get the chance to redo or undo these formative weeks.

How responsive your dog is to you, how she gets along with other dogs and people of all types, and how easy she is to live with will be largely determined by what you do before your puppy is six months old.

It will be up to you, with help from many resources, to do what it takes to have your puppy develop into the wonderful adult companion you had in mind. Your veterinarian will teach you how to keep your puppy healthy through proper diet, dental care, exercise, regular veterinary exams and vaccinations. Keeping your dog's weight within certain limits, checking her teeth and gums to be sure they are clean and not inflamed, making sure her coat is clean and free from mats, and keeping her nails comfortably short are all signs you are maintaining your puppy in good physical health. We'll introduce you to these topics in the next chapter.

 ## What is Behavior Wellness?

But what about your puppy's behavioral health? Do you know the signs that indicate your puppy is behaviorally healthy? This is a new concept for most puppy owners and professionals alike. You may tend to judge your puppy's behavior based on the _absence_ of problems, rather than from the _presence_ of desirable behaviors.

As a new puppy owner you may be thinking, "I don't want her to pee on the carpet," or, "I don't want her to bark at the neighbors." From the standpoint of behavioral health, instead you'll think, "I want her to relieve herself outside," or "I want her to be friendly but quiet when she sees the neighbors." Describing your puppy's behavior based on characteristics you **do** want, rather than ones you don't, is a wellness perspective.

Having a behavior wellness perspective means defining normal and acceptable behaviors you want your puppy to have, implementing concrete training and management plans which will help your puppy develop these behavioral habits, continually paying attention to the status of your puppy's behavioral health, and knowing how to get help when you need it.

If you are taking care of your puppy's behavioral health, you aren't waiting until problems develop to take action. Every day you are taking steps to help your puppy develop healthy behavior patterns.

But how do we define the healthy behavior patterns you are striving for? How do we describe a behaviorally healthy dog?

Characteristics of Behaviorally Healthy Dogs

As your puppy grows up, somehow she just won't passively turn into the companion you want. You have to describe how you want your dog to behave, so you can then discover what you need to do to encourage those behaviors.

To help you get started, we've provided a list of good behaviors that most people want from their dogs, and behaviors that make your dog a safe and enjoyable member of your community. We've taken into account what we can realistically expect from our canine companions, given what's normal behavior for dogs. We've also provided an overview of your role in molding those behaviors.

Behaviorally Healthy Dogs:

Are affectionate without being "needy"

A behaviorally healthy dog is bonded to the family, but can amuse herself without constantly demanding attention. Spend quality time with your puppy, and behave in a trustworthy and predictable fashion so a strong bond of companionship develops between the two of you. Avoid reinforcing annoying, pestering behaviors by ignoring them and instead teach your puppy to sit, lie down, or wait quietly to get your attention. You should also pay attention to your puppy when she isn't pestering you.

Are friendly toward friendly people and well-behaved children

Socialize your puppy by letting her have many pleasant experiences with people of different sizes and ages, wearing all kinds of clothing, with beards, glasses, unusual gaits, as well as assistive devices like canes and wheelchairs. Pay particular attention to socializing your puppy to children of all ages. Read more about how to do this in Chapter 3. The importance of socialization cannot be overemphasized.

Get along with other friendly dogs, including dogs outside the family

Dogs must begin learning their social skills during puppyhood. Play sessions during puppy classes are a great place to start. Continue to socialize your puppy through adolescence, and into adulthood so she can maintain good social skills by being around other friendly dogs.

Off-leash play sessions in safe places are better than those on tight leashes. If the only encounters your puppy has with other dogs is when she's straining at the leash or being threatened by dogs behind fences, she'll quickly learn that other dogs mean either frustration or intimidation for her.

If you want your puppy to be good with cats, birds, horses or other animals, you must socialize her to them as well.

Are at ease with normal, everyday handling

This includes having feet wiped, nails trimmed, mouth opened, and being petted and touched anywhere on the body. Gradually accustom your puppy to these procedures using gentle techniques and lots of "good things" such as tidbits and toys as described later in this book.

Can be left alone for reasonable time periods in the house or yard without becoming anxious or panicked

Gradually accustom your puppy to being alone. Start with short time periods of 10 minutes or so. It is not a good idea to adopt a new puppy one day, and leave for an entire workday the next. If you use a crate for your puppy, you must take the time to gradually acclimate her to it, over several days or a week (refer to Chapter 5).

Relieve themselves only in desired areas

This could be a yard, on leash walks, or even in a doggie litterbox, depending on your living arrangements. Use appropriate housetraining procedures, which do not involve discipline or punishment, and give your dog enough opportunities and suitable locations for relieving herself (see Chapter 6).

Are not overly fearful of normal, everyday events or new things

This requires socialization, which you'll learn more about later, ideally beginning in puppyhood, to help prevent fear-related problems. Do not punish fear-related behaviors, or force your puppy to experience what she is afraid of. Instead, let her do things at her own pace with lots of enjoyable enticements such as food and toys.

Can adapt to change with minimal problems

Help your puppy be resilient in times of change through training and socialization, and planning for her needs when lifestyle changes such as moving, vacations, or the birth of a baby occur.

Play well with people and other dogs by not becoming uncontrollable or rough

Encourage acceptable play behaviors such as fetching. Even tug of war is OK, as long as your puppy never puts teeth to skin and relinquishes the toy when asked. Do not encourage your puppy to use your body parts as play toys, by batting your puppy around her face, enticing her to chase or nip your fingers, or allowing her to grab your ankles.

Play with their own toys, and are not often destructive

Make sure your puppy has enough toys of different types—some to chew, others to fetch and carry, and others to shake and tug. Consider your puppy's personal preferences for what she likes.

Are content when left in a yard, car or crate for reasonable time periods and do not try to escape or threaten people passing by

Securely contain your puppy on your property using humane methods and do not tie your puppy out. Gradually acclimate her to crating and being left alone and encourage friendly, rather than territorial behavior. You'll learn more about how to accomplish these goals as you read through this book.

Reliably respond when told to sit, down, come or stay and can walk nicely on a loose leash

Teach your puppy these behaviors using humane training techniques based on positive reinforcement (see Chapter 12). Practice in many different situations, including when your puppy is distracted by other things such as wanting to chase a squirrel, so your puppy will learn to perform these behaviors no matter where you are.

Bark when appropriate, but not to excess

Barking and other vocalizations are normal communication behaviors for dogs. Provide a quality environment so nuisance barking due to boredom, fear or other reasons does not occur.

Readily relinquish control of food, toys and other objects

Teach your puppy that giving up control of these items is a good thing to do because a reward will follow.

Calm down and recover quickly if startled, frightened or excited

Socialization helps prevent dogs from becoming overwhelmed in excitable situations. Encourage your puppy to sit or lie down when she becomes too excited, or give her a quick "time out." Avoid yelling as this only heightens her arousal.

 Breed and Individual Differences

The Behaviorally Healthy Dog Criteria apply regardless of your puppy's breed. Certain behaviors may be easier or more difficult to elicit, depending on your puppy's breed. It may be easy to teach a Labrador retriever to be friendly, but more difficult to teach her to calm down when excited. It may be just the opposite for an Akita.

Breed tendencies are important, but learning and experience have just as much, if not more, effect on your puppy's behavior. More accurately, your puppy's environmental experiences interact with her breed tendencies to determine her behavioral characteristics.

The remainder of this book will guide you on how to give your puppy the behavioral nurturing she needs to bring out her best natural tendencies.

 The Five-Step Positive Proaction Plan:
A Blueprint for a Behaviorally Healthy Dog

While raising a puppy is a big responsibility and requires an investment of time and energy, it also has big payoffs. Your dog can be your best friend and enrich your life in ways that even your best human friend or family member may not.

As you read through the behaviorally healthy characteristics, you might be thinking, "Gee—there's so much for me to do, I don't know where to start!"

Helping your puppy grow up behaviorally healthy is not as difficult as you might think. To help get your puppy started on the road to behavioral health, you need a plan. You need a few guiding principles that will help you mold your puppy's behaviors into behaviorally healthy patterns.

What should you do when your puppy jumps on people? Should you show your puppy her "mess" if she urinates on the floor? What about when you catch your puppy chewing on the couch? We could list a thousand different questions you'll have, and you'd still have more.

Use our Five-Step Positive Proaction Plan–your guiding principles–to help you know what to do with each of these normal puppy behaviors. Because every puppy's situation is just a little different, by using this Plan rather than relying on "cookbook" answers found in other books, you have the flexibility of thinking through how to select and apply the steps to _your_ puppy.

If you are unsure how to do so, that's a sign you need to contact your veterinarian or animal shelter for a referral to a certified trainer or animal behaviorist. Guidelines on what qualifications and experience to look for from these experts are included in Chapter 14.

Step 1: Help Your Puppy Do the Right Thing

The first step in having a behaviorally healthy dog is to **catch your puppy doing something right.** When your puppy eliminates outside for example, reward her _immediately._ If your puppy finally lies down and is quietly chewing on her toy, gently pet her and tell her what a good dog she is. Catching your puppy doing something right is like taking advantage of "teachable moments" to let her know that you like what she's doing. Good behavior too often goes unrewarded. Reinforcement can be a tidbit, playing with your puppy, or quietly petting her. Dogs who are unruly, annoying and pester people, often receive the most attention when they are misbehaving, and do not receive sufficient reinforcement for good behaviors. If you seldom reinforce your puppy when she is quiet and calm, and doing what you want, you may be making it more likely your puppy will discover that misbehavior has a better payoff.

At other times, you may need to be *proactive* and take steps to trigger the behavior you want. Reinforcement only makes good behavior more likely to occur. You must also actively draw out the behavior you want so you can reinforce it. There are several easy ways to do this.

One is a technique called "lure-reward." A lure is something that prompts your puppy to do what you want. For example, you could teach your puppy to come by showing her a treat, or shaking the container that holds the treats. When she comes, you give her the tidbit (the reward). Once she has the idea, you can fade out the treat as a lure, and *only* use it for a reward after she comes. You'll find more details about teaching specific behaviors later in this book.

You can also use the lure-reward method to teach your puppy to enjoy being rolled over, gently restrained and "giving in" to you. Your puppy shouldn't resist or be afraid of these positions. Putting your puppy in these positions in a confrontational, threatening manner only frightens her and makes her dislike these procedures. By luring your puppy into these positions, you can create an expectation that doing these things is fun and enjoyable. Procedures such as nail trimming, brushing, and cleaning feet can also be paired with tidbits and toys. How to introduce your puppy to these procedures is discussed in Chapter 11.

 ## Step 2: Keep Bad Habits from Developing

Managing your puppy's environment so she doesn't have the chance to do the wrong thing is an essential step in the Plan. Your job is to make it easy for your puppy to do what you want her to do, and very difficult to do the things you don't like.

Puppies are curious and inquisitive creatures and will undoubtedly get into something they shouldn't if someone isn't watching. You need to know what your puppy is doing almost every second. Your puppy should never be out of your sight long enough to get herself into trouble by relieving herself inside or chewing on things she shouldn't.

For general management during puppy housetraining and the destructive young dog phase, baby gates, tethering your puppy to you, and closing doors are all helpful. So is puppy-proofing the house, by putting as many items as you can out of your puppy's reach.

Crate training, which is a very useful option for puppies, is discussed in Chapter 5. Other types of management include having a leash and treats ready at the door to prevent door dashing and jumping on people, and using a Gentle Leader® head collar to prevent leash pulling while teaching your puppy to walk on a loose leash.

Puppies don't learn what is "right" or "wrong." What they learn is to repeat behaviors that have pleasant consequences, and to avoid doing things that make bad things happen. Behavior that "works," by allowing your puppy to accomplish a goal, relieve frustration or stress, or meet a need, will continue, and will become a "habit"–either good or bad.

If your puppy can bark and successfully get your attention, she learns barking is what she should do when she wants something. Don't be trapped into giving your puppy what she wants to stop annoying or embarrassing behavior. If you never reward these behaviors, your puppy will stop doing them.

Instead, teach your puppy what **to do** when she wants something from you. One way to do this is to have your puppy respond to a cue such as, "sit," "down," "shake hands," etc., before receiving things she wants, such as being petted, played with, let outside, put on leash for a walk, etc.

This pattern creates an expectation for your puppy that responding to these cues predicts "good things" will happen. By establishing "good habits," we are preventing "bad ones" from developing.

🦴 Step 3: Meet Your Puppy's Behavioral and Developmental Needs

It will be easier for your puppy to be a well-behaved companion if you meet her behavioral needs. Behavioral needs are things that a dog must have to behave in a normal way. For example, you won't be able to housetrain your puppy if you don't give her enough opportunities to relieve herself outside. If your puppy doesn't have either enough chew toys, or the right kind, don't be surprised if she begins chewing the furniture. Opportunities to chew, eliminate and play are all behavioral needs in dogs. Trying to prevent these behaviors from happening will only create problems for you and your dog. How to meet these needs will be discussed in detail in later sections.

Perhaps the most important developmental need puppies have is the need for socialization. Early in life, it is vitally important that your puppy learn to treat people and other animals as friends, and learn how to adapt to new things and situations.

Socialization is not an automatic process, but one you must put considerable time and energy into. While young puppies may be very friendly because they are generally not fearful, without socialization, this openness will NOT persist into adulthood.

Puppies who do not have enough experience with all different types of people and different animals, places and things, will grow up to be fearful of or aggressive toward anything new and different. You'll learn more about how to socialize your puppy in Chapter 3.

Puppies also need a safe, comfortable place to sleep. It should be out of the main traffic of the house but not isolated from the family. Your puppy should have the freedom to go to her sleep spot whenever she wishes. For many puppies a crate may be the first sleep spot they have.

Dogs also need to have freedom from unnecessary pain, fear and distress. Monitor your puppy's responses to her world and remove her from things that scare or hurt her. You may wonder about the word "unnecessary." Unfortunately some pain, fear or distress can be necessary. For example, your puppy may feel each of these things when she's vaccinated, but only for a short time. The benefit of the vaccinations outweighs the momentary pain, fear or distress your puppy may experience.

Dogs need to have some control over their environment. They need to feel that they can control events such as when they can lie down, get a drink of water or stretch. Puppies aren't ready for as much freedom or control over their environment as adult dogs. In fact, controlling some aspects of their environment helps with housetraining, destructiveness and socialization.

Pleasant social contact with people or other dogs is an important need of dogs. If you are socializing your puppy correctly, you should be meeting those needs. Be sure to continue to provide this contact as your puppy gets older.

Dogs need exercise and mental stimulation. Socialization experiences, walks, play periods and training should help provide these needs for your puppy. Think about how you will meet these needs on a regular basis as your puppy grows to adulthood. Learn more about socialization in Chapter 3. Basic needs for physical health are discussed in Chapter 2.

 ### Step 4: Use the "Take-Away" Method to Discourage Behaviors You Don't Like

There are two main ways to decrease behaviors you don't like. One is to follow the behavior with something aversive ("discipline"); which is anything your puppy will work to avoid. The other is to take away something desirable when your puppy performs the unwanted behavior.

Get in the habit of using the "take-away" method, and you will avoid many of the problems aversives can create. The trick to using this method successfully is to know what your puppy wants and be able to control her access to it.

In addition, the "good thing" must be taken away *immediately* following the behavior and must be taken away *every time* she does the unwanted behavior. Any delay or inconsistency will result in failure.

After the take-away, give your puppy another chance to do the right behavior so the thing she wants can be returned to her. You'll learn more about the "take-away" method in the sections of this book that deal with specific unwanted behaviors, but the following examples will help you get the idea.

Behavior	What To Take Away
nipping at hands	chance to play with you–walk away
pulling on the leash	chance to keep moving forward–stop, stand still
jumping up	chance to be petted–turn your back or leave the room
attacking your ankles	chance to be with you–put puppy in a small, dark room for a few minutes, or someplace else she doesn't want to be
playing roughly	chance to play–take toy away, stop playing and walk away

A time out is one type of take-away method. With this method, you are taking away your puppy's chance to receive any reward for the un-wanted behavior.

Let's say your puppy jumps on you for attention. As in the example above, you turn and walk away from your puppy. You can even go into another room and shut the door for a few minutes. Jumping up causes the puppy to lose her chance at getting attention, because you have left her. You'll learn more about this technique in later sections.

 ## Step 5: Make Discipline the Last Resort and Use it Correctly

The word "discipline" is a vague term with many different meanings. Because a wellness approach focuses on you helping your puppy learn to do the *right* thing, discipline is the last tool in your toolbox, not the first. Even when used correctly, which is very difficult to do, the most discipline can accomplish is to teach your puppy what *not* to do. The most important part of training is teaching your puppy what *to do.*

Using the wrong type of discipline can result in your puppy being afraid of you, your hands, or anything in the surrounding environment your puppy associates with this unpleasant treatment. The more unpleasant the experience, especially if it causes pain, the greater the likelihood for these harmful side effects.

Usually the best use of discipline is when it is an automatic and immediate consequence of your puppy's behavior, in the form of "booby traps," or remote punishment. Remote punishment is either triggered directly by your puppy's behavior, or is something that you can activate at a distance, without touching your puppy. Examples include an SSSCat®, a motion detector that sprays a harmless mist when activated, or a Snappy Trainer®, a harmless, modified mousetrap that flies into the air when triggered. Both are available from our Web site at www.AnimalBehaviorAssociates.com, or see the Order Form at the back of this book.

To be effective, "discipline" must be consistent and immediate. Never ever try to punish your puppy for behavior you didn't see her do. Because it's unlikely you'll catch every occurrence of the unwanted behavior, discipline is less effective than you might think.

You'll find that merely interrupting an unwanted behavior and replacing it with a desirable one is a better choice. For example, if you catch your puppy chewing on the sofa, clap your hands to interrupt her, and then direct her attention to a chewie of her own.

 ## Monitoring Your Puppy's Behavioral Health

Now that you know the behavioral goals you are working toward, it is much easier for you to keep tabs on how your puppy is doing behaviorally. In the same way that you monitor your puppy's physical health by keeping an eye on her weight, noticing when her nails need trimming, when she needs brushing or a bath, you must also monitor your puppy's behavioral health.

It is human nature to make excuses, rationalize, or ignore signs that your puppy's behavior may be changing in unwanted ways. Maybe your previously friendly puppy is now barking threateningly at visitors. Perhaps your puppy and adult dog that used to get along reasonably well are now growling and snapping at each other. Maybe you thought your puppy was housetrained, but is now relieving herself inside and "forgetting" to let you know she needs to go outside. It's tempting to take a "wait and see" approach and hope things will get better.

This gambling approach is fraught with dangers. While it is possible that your puppy's behavior may improve on its own, it is much more likely it won't. The longer they continue, the easier it becomes for unwanted behaviors to become habits and more difficult to change.

Behavior changes can be triggered by changes in your family's routine or living circumstances. You may be able to prevent problems if you proactively consider your puppy's needs during family changes such as the following:

- Change in family's routine or schedule, if for example a person returns to work
  · can trigger separation anxiety or "boredom" destructive behavior

- Change in family composition, with a new baby, or change in roommates
  · can trigger territorial or other threatening behaviors as well as urine-marking

- Move to a new home
  · can trigger separation anxiety or urine-marking

- Vacation, with your puppy either being boarded or traveling with you
  · your puppy needs to be acclimated to traveling, including crate training, or to the boarding kennel with brief visits before you leave her

- Addition or loss of another pet
  · can trigger relationship changes between the remaining pets or separation anxiety

- Illness in the family, causing a change in time available to care for the puppy
  · your puppy can become destructive or begin soiling if her needs for play, exercise and chances to relieve herself aren't being met

Work with your veterinarian and a certified behaviorist or trainer to help you monitor your puppy's behavior.

Getting Help when Problems Arise

It is to your benefit, and certainly your puppy's, to get help for problem behaviors sooner not later. The last thing you want is for your puppy's quality of life to decrease as a result of restrictions on her activities because of unwanted behavior.

You can begin to think less of your puppy when her behavior becomes dangerous, destructive or annoying. These kinds of changes put your relationship with your puppy at risk. No one wants your puppy to have to find another home.

When you need behavioral help, you may be confused about where to go. The first step is to contact your veterinarian. Some behavior problems or changes, particularly housesoiling and aggression, can have medical causes. It is important to be sure that nothing is medically wrong with your puppy before seeking behavioral assistance. Your veterinarian can help you find a behavior consultant. Use the guidelines on this subject, found in Chapter 14, to help you.

 ## Attitude is All Important

The last thing to keep in mind when implementing these behavior wellness principles is that puppies and adult dogs are not vindictive, rebellious, spiteful or guilty. They simply do what works for them. If you are tempted to explain your puppy's behavior with these anthropomorphic intentions (applying human motivations to animals), **STOP** and reinterpret the situation from your puppy's point of view.

For example, "guilty" looks are nothing more than submissive behaviors because your puppy feels threatened by you. What you think are "spiteful" behaviors such as tearing things up when left alone are often due to separation anxiety, or simply because your puppy is bored and has a good time doing it.

Try to understand the behavior from your puppy's point of view rather than jumping to interpretations that make more sense for people than for dogs. Keep a positive attitude of, "How can I get her to do what I want so I can reward her." Review the Five-Step Plan and find help right away if you are "stuck" and don't know what to do next.

Chapter 2
Wellness Care for Your Puppy's Physical Health

Your puppy's behavior and mental well-being depend on his physical health. Sickness, poor nutrition, and various physical disorders adversely impact his ability to learn and thrive. Sometimes unacceptable behaviors can be traced to health problems. Resolving the health problem takes care of the behavior issue.

Some health problems appear early in life, even before you bring your puppy home. As an example, intestinal parasites (worms) can infect puppies before and shortly after birth. Diarrhea and upset stomach are possible results of parasite infection, impeding successful house training.

This chapter provides crucial information you need about your puppy's physical health from a *prevention* perspective. Preventive health care is less expensive than treating medical problems once they occur.

Because preventive medicine protocols change due to ongoing scientific research, the health care information in this chapter is only a guideline. New information, as well as your puppy's breed and individual characteristics, will influence your veterinarian's recommendations.

Customized Wellness Visits for Your Puppy–When

As soon as you know when you'll be bringing your puppy home, schedule his first appointment with your veterinarian. Bring all health care records your puppy's original caretakers can provide.

Your veterinarian will help you plan a preventive health care program. Physical exams can start at six weeks of age. Veterinarians generally recommend reexaminations every four weeks, until at least twelve weeks of age. Another physical exam will often be done just before your puppy is spayed or neutered (four to six months of age).

Ask your veterinarian for advice about a *lifelong* strategy of regular wellness care that goes beyond the early puppy visits when required vaccinations are administered. The first seven months of life are particularly important and many veterinarians now recommend physical wellness exams twice a year for maximizing the probability of early detection and treatment of disease.

Customized Wellness Visits for Your Puppy– What to Expect

These first wellness visits are packed with information and procedures. Be ready to write down information your veterinary staff will provide, and come prepared with questions.

Your veterinarian will interview you about your puppy's background and care, and may request that you complete a basic health questionnaire. He will give your puppy a physical examination that evaluates all body systems. The purpose of this exam is to detect problems early. Your veterinarian looks for evidence of disease and abnormalities such as congenital (developmental) and genetic (inherited) defects, considering risk factors associated with the breed of your puppy.

Your veterinarian should explain all the results from the examination, and may summarize them on a take-home checklist. Make sure your veterinarian gives you specific recommendations for any abnormal findings. Sometimes your veterinarian will simply recommend rechecking the problem in a few weeks. For example, a heart murmur detected at six weeks of age may improve or even resolve itself as your puppy grows. Keep asking questions of your veterinary staff until you fully understand the health care plan for your puppy.

Unusual behavior or changes in behavior can sometimes be symptoms of illness. Discuss them with the medical staff. If you are uncertain what normal behaviors are, ask. Like physical problems, behavior issues should be addressed as early as possible, if not prevented altogether.

 ## Wellness through Prevention of Contagious Diseases

Your puppy is susceptible to a variety of diseases, some of which can be prevented by appropriate vaccinations. Some diseases, such as rabies, can be transmitted to people and are called *zoonoses.* Preventing zoonoses is another important reason for regular preventive care through veterinary wellness examinations.

In general, commercially available vaccinations are highly effective against the diseases they were designed to prevent and are safe for most puppies. However, no vaccine will be effective and safe in 100% of cases. Your veterinarian will recommend the best schedule of vaccinations for your puppy based on the latest scientific information and the environmental risk factors specific to your area.

Vaccines for distemper, hepatitis, parainfluenza and parvovirus are given at approximately four week intervals, from six to twelve weeks of age. A booster vaccination is given one year after the final puppy shot, then every three years thereafter. Your veterinarian may recommend a different protocol for your puppy based on individual factors.

Because it is so deadly, rabies vaccination frequency is dictated by state law. After an initial vaccination at twelve weeks and a booster at twelve months, a booster every three years or sooner is required by law.

Your veterinarian may recommend other vaccines based on your puppy's activities, environment and health status. For example, if you frequently walk your puppy in deer tick infested areas, your veterinarian will likely recommend your puppy be vaccinated against Lyme Disease.

 ## Wellness through Parasite Control

Parasites can be internal or external. They may cause health problems for your puppy by migrating through and damaging multiple internal organs, or they may carry other diseases.

Parasite prevention and control is a top health priority not only for your puppy, but to prevent people from becoming infected as well. Some parasites can cause serious disease in people, especially children and those with impaired immune systems.

Canine roundworm eggs present a special threat to children. If ingested, the eggs hatch and migrate abnormally, sometimes to the eye, causing blindness. See Box 2-1 for steps to protect your child against this common and dangerous parasite. For both your puppy's and your family's well-being, we cannot overemphasize the importance of fecal screening for your puppy.

Your puppy's first veterinary wellness exam should include analysis of his feces to screen for microscopic worm eggs. Because a single negative result without eggs does *not* mean your puppy is not infected, your veterinarian may recommend multiple fecal parasite screenings. If you observe diarrhea, poorly formed stool, or blood or mucous mixed with the stool, collect it in a plastic bag and take it to your veterinarian for analysis, as any of these signs can indicate a parasite problem.

Of all parasitic diseases, heartworm is probably the most dangerous, especially in areas with high mosquito populations, as this insect carries the parasite. Heartworm medication is started at about seven weeks of age. Your veterinarian will determine if a blood test will be required before medication can be given and how often the test should be repeated, in accordance with guidelines from the American Heartworm Society, www.heartwormsociety.org.

Fleas not only cause skin and coat problems but also carry tapeworms. Ticks carry many serious diseases that can be extremely debilitating or fatal, including Rocky Mountain Spotted Fever, Ehrlichiosis and Lyme's Disease.

Today's preventive products greatly reduce the risk of infection to both pets and people by these parasites. Your veterinarian may prescribe a single medication which protects your puppy from a wide variety of parasitic diseases. Because parasite threats vary by region, your veterinarian will recommend products that provide the best protection for your puppy's circumstances. Ask your veterinarian about products to use in your yard and elsewhere to keep flea populations under control.

Protecting Children from Roundworm Infection
▼ Ensure all puppy fecal material is promptly picked up and properly disposed of
▼ If the puppy soils itself, bathe it promptly
▼ Wash the puppy's bedding every few days, or more often if necessary
▼ Always wash your hands after handling the puppy, its fecal material, its bedding, or other items that might be contaminated
▼ Always wash your hands before eating
▼ Always wash your hands after gardening, working or playing in areas where dogs frequent
▼ Teach children to not put their hands, toys or other objects in their mouths

Box 2.1

 ## Wellness through Skin and Hair Care

The hair coat protects the skin and body from wounds, the environment (sun, cold, heat, wind), and insects; however, a dog's thick coat can hide problems. Regular combing and brushing of your puppy's hair coat and inspection of his body helps promote good health by spotting problems early such as:

- Skin and feet infections, cuts, sores and other lesions
- Inflammation between skin folds
- Ear inflammation (redness, discharge, itching, head shaking)

- Overly long nails that cause discomfort and affect the shape of the foot
- Ticks and fleas before they attach firmly to the skin
- Bumps, lumps and skin growths
- Redness of, or discharge from, the eyes
- Mouth problems including retained, crooked, or broken teeth and inflamed gums (see dental health section)

In long-hair breeds, grooming and hair cuts may be needed every six to eight weeks. You can trim your dog's hair coat or use a professional groomer. An expert groomer should inform you about possible skin and coat problems identified during the grooming process. You'll want to acclimate your puppy to the grooming salon early, rather than waiting until he actually needs a hair cut or bath.

Ask a professional groomer or your veterinarian about the best grooming equipment for your puppy's needs. For example, you should use a toenail clipper designed for dogs that has new, sharp blades. Never use a clipper with dull blades as they will pinch and hurt your puppy, causing him to resist nail trimming.

When you brush, comb and massage your puppy's coat and skin on a daily basis, you teach him to trust and enjoy being touched everywhere and relax when physically handled and restrained. Think how you feel when getting a massage!

Grooming sessions can be "bonding time" for you and your puppy. Regular grooming will help your puppy be more amenable to handling during other situations such as veterinary visits. As you'll see in Chapter 11, you do not need, and should not use force, nor be an "alpha" to have your puppy accept and enjoy being groomed and touched.

Grooming time also gives you the opportunity to practice basic behaviors such as "sit" and "down." See Chapter 12 for details on teaching these and other basic behaviors.

 ## Wellness through Good Nutrition

Find out from whomever you acquired your puppy what they have been feeding him and ask for several portions to take with you until you can buy your own food. Your veterinarian may likely recommend a specific food depending on the size your puppy will grow to be and other factors. If you need to change food, do so gradually by mixing small portions of the new food with your puppy's current food. Over a few days, feed less of the current food and more of the new diet. This will prevent diarrhea and other signs of intestinal distress.

In general, you get what you pay for when it comes to dog food. Very inexpensive food is often manufactured from lower quality, less fresh ingredients that are poorly digested and absorbed. Freshness is important for optimal vitamin and nutrient quality. High quality foods will be more expensive on a per pound basis, however, they provide better absorption and efficiency per ounce fed, so you can feed smaller portions. This leads to fewer messes to clean up in your yard and on walks.

It can be confusing to choose a food from the many excellent commercially prepared diets, so ask your veterinarian at the first puppy visit. As your puppy matures, you will adjust feeding times and diet type per recommendations from your veterinarian and the food manufacturer.

Raw food diets for pets have become increasingly popular. Be aware that raw foods may be contaminated with disease agents, most often E. coli and salmonella, which could cause dire illness in your puppy, as they do in people. Discuss the pros and cons of raw diets with your veterinarian before taking the plunge.

Chocolate, raisins, raw onions and other foods, as well as some houseplants, are toxic to dogs. Ask your veterinarian for a list of dangerous substances, or contact the ASPCA's Animal Poison Control Center at 888-426-4435 or www.apcc.aspca.org.

Obesity
With the many excellent and very palatable foods available, pet obesity is a chief concern. Too much food and too little exercise is as much a problem for dogs as it is for humans. Don't let your puppy get fat–it's easier to keep weight off than to take it off once obesity is a problem. Restrict "people food" and treats to training sessions as too much of these contribute to obesity and poor general health. To prevent begging, avoid feeding your pet from your plate.

Training Treats: Tiny and Tasty
Food rewards are valuable training tools so make the treats you use special rather than giving them to your puppy "for free." Choose treats that can be cut into bite-size morsels, be swallowed quickly without much chewing, and aren't too messy to put in your training pouch or pocket. You may even want to use a portion of your puppy's daily meals for training so you can keep him at optimum weight.

There are many commercial treats that meet the above criteria. Consider liver based tidbits, treats made for cats, or some "people food" such as tiny pieces of hard cheese or hot dogs. Low calorie options include small pieces of raw carrots, apples, fresh green beans (yes, many dogs like these crunchy pieces) or even dry cereal.

Wellness through Good Dental Health

Many dental diseases and problems can be prevented through regular dental care. At every wellness exam your veterinarian should check your puppy's oral health and bring to your attention any signs of disease.

Your veterinarian will recommend extraction of any abnormally retained baby (deciduous) teeth to prevent infection and diseased tissues around permanent teeth. This can be accomplished when your puppy is spayed or neutered.

Between professional checkups you should routinely examine your puppy's teeth and gums (see Wellness through Skin and Hair Care). You can also take an active role in your puppy's dental health by regularly brushing his teeth. Use toothbrushes and pastes designed for dogs. See Chapter 11 for procedures on accustoming your puppy to having his teeth brushed.

As your puppy gets older he will need periodic routine teeth cleaning and polishing to prevent infection of the gums and bones around the teeth (called periodontal disease). These procedures are performed by your veterinarian with your dog under anesthesia.

Your puppy will need safe items to chew on while he is teething, to help keep his teeth clean and to meet his behavioral need to chew.

Although there is always debate on the subject, regular chewing on raw beef bones is very effective for keeping teeth clean and stimulating healthy gums. The risks are broken teeth (cooked bones shouldn't be given for this reason as they are much harder and more brittle than raw bones). Enzymatically enhanced rawhides and other chew toys designed to promote dental health are a good option. See Chapter 8 for more suggestions on appropriate chew toys.

Wellness through Reproductive Health

Behavior and general physical health are enhanced by early sterilization. In the male dog, sexual sterilization surgery (castration or neuter) removes both testicles, the source of male sex hormones. Female dogs undergo a complete ovariohysterectomy (spay or neuter), the medical term for removal of the ovaries and uterus. The ovaries are the source of female sex hormones, while the uterus can be a source of disease later in life.

Neuter surgeries should be done around four to six months of age, before your puppy becomes sexually mature. A female dog should *not* have a heat period (time of sexual receptivity) before she is neutered. Many recent studies support the benefits of pediatric neutering–spaying and castration at a relatively young age (16 weeks).

There are so many good reasons for spaying and neutering, it is impossible to make an argument against them.

Benefits of Spaying and Neutering
▶ Spaying and neutering have a positive affect on the pet overpopulation problem, and decrease the number of physically healthy pets that are euthanized in shelters because no one wants them
▶ Dogs can become sexually mature and active as early as six to seven months of age, resulting in early and unexpected pregnancies
▶ According to various bite statistics, intact male dogs are more likely to bite than neutered male or female dogs[1]
▶ Neutering reduces the frequency of urine-marking, roaming and mounting in male dogs[2]
▶ Older, sexually intact females are more prone to mammary cancer and uterine disease than are spayed females. Intact male dogs have a higher incidence of prostatic disease and complications arising from it, as well as testicular cancer
▶ Raising pure-bred dogs is not a "get rich quick" scheme
▶ It is irresponsible to allow your dog to birth puppies for the reason of providing your child "an experience"
[1] Lockwood, L. 1995. The ethology and epidemiology of canine aggression. Pps. 131-138 in J. Serpell, Ed. The Domestic Dog. Cambridge University Press. [2] Hopkins, S.G., et.al. 1976. Castration of adult male dogs. Effects on roaming, aggression, urine marking, and mounting. JAVMA 168: 1108-10.

Box 2.2

 ## Wellness through Environmental Management

Pups love to explore the world with their mouths. Keeping your puppy well and safe is much like planning safekeeping for a two-year-old.

You'll want to "puppy-proof" your house much like you would to create a safe environment for a toddler. Keep small objects that could cause choking or intestinal blockages if ingested, and poisonous substances such as antifreeze and prescription medications out of reach or securely put away. Supervise interactions between your puppy and other pets or children as described in Chapters 3 and 7, and train him to stay in a crate when left alone for reasonably short periods, as described in Chapter 5.

Although your puppy belongs inside the house with you most of the time, you must also provide a safe outdoor environment. Your puppy needs a confined area with a secure fence, as you must NOT leave your puppy tied out or tethered. More and more communities are passing laws restricting tethering, or banning it altogether.

Your puppy should only be off-leash in an approved off-leash area and only after he is reliably trained to come to you when called and to STOP on command.

NEVER allow your puppy to ride unrestrained in the open bed of a truck. Curious or frightened puppies can leap out or be thrown out when you stop or swerve quickly. Your puppy is also at risk of having dirt and debris fly into his eyes. Place your puppy in a well-secured crate in the truck bed, put him in the cab, or leave him safely at home.

Identification
Your puppy must carry identification so that he can be reunited with you if he gets lost. Most veterinarians provide microchip implanting services, which we strongly recommend. The chip is easily implanted when your puppy is anesthetized for spaying or neutering.

Ensure the chip brand being implanted is universally recognized by the scanners used by humane shelters, animal control agencies and veterinary offices. Your puppy's information won't be on file with the national registry until you mail in the required registration forms or complete them on-line.

In addition to a microchip, keep a collar on your puppy that holds local license and rabies tags. A personal ID tag with your puppy's name and your contact information to serve as a backup for his microchip is a good idea.

Be very choosey about the collar you leave on your puppy for identification purposes as hanging is still a risk with a buckle or snap-release collar. For this reason, we strongly recommend the KeepSafe Break-Away collar (www.keepsafecollar.com) available at Premier™ Pet Products (www.premier.com). This innovatively designed collar includes a clasp that will release if enough pressure is put on it. Your puppy should NEVER be left unsupervised wearing a choke or prong collar, and because we don't recommend these collars for training, your puppy doesn't need them.

 ## Wellness through Regular Exercise

Your puppy needs plenty of exercise to develop into a behaviorally healthy and physically fit dog. Even so, too much of a good thing can be bad. Exposing young bone growth plates and joints to strenuous exercise or very rough play sessions can lead to injury and permanent damage, especially in large breed dogs.

Talk with your veterinarian about the limits of what your puppy is capable of doing. Use common sense. Overexerting baby joints may cause injury leading to arthritis, gait abnormalities and permanent lameness.

In general, exercise in controlled situations like walking on leash is safe and can hardly be overdone. Swimming also provides excellent muscle toning and aerobic workout without undue stress on joints and bones for dogs of all ages. Be sure to acclimate your puppy to water gradually, without force, and only allow him to swim in areas where you can rescue him if he panics.

 ## Budgeting Pet Wellness Care

Veterinary care is a bargain compared to human medicine. Even so, an ounce of prevention is worth a pound of cure. By committing to *preventing* problems before they occur, you can avoid some large veterinary bills later in your puppy's life. Staying current with regular wellness exams and medical care is always less expensive–financially and emotionally–than treating a disease or injury that could have been prevented.

Remember that owning a pet is a responsibility, not a right. By adopting a puppy, you are making a lifelong commitment to a living, intelligent and loving creature. You'll never regret the choice, as long as you give your full effort to raising him the right way.

Chapter 3
Socialization: What It is and Why It is Important to You and Your Puppy

 ## What is Socialization?

You may have heard about the importance of socializing your puppy. But what does this really mean? The answer is not as simple as you might think.

The term "socialization" was first defined in the scientific literature, and refers to the creation of social bonds or attachments to other individuals. The first social bonds your puppy forms are to her mom and littermates. Early on, puppies also need to form bonds with people.

Socialization, sometimes called social learning, can also describe how young animals learn normal social behavior, and how to behave toward others. Social learning occurs when your puppy plays and interacts with other puppies, people and other animals.

She learns, among other things, how to be friendly, not only to puppies, but also to people, cats and other animals she is exposed to. She learns the consequences of being too rough, what happens if she threatens others, and what to do when others threaten her.

Puppies also learn by assuming different roles in their relationships, sometimes being assertive and confident, and other times being submissive and "giving in."

In the popular literature, socialization refers to the process of giving your puppy pleasant experiences with many different kinds of people, all kinds of places, other animals, and everyday events and objects.

It can also refer to the end result of this process. A well-socialized dog can accept change and enjoys having new experiences, is friendly to people and other animals, and isn't frightened by new environments or things she hasn't seen or done before.

Good socialization during puppyhood has a critical effect on your dog's adult behavior. It is one of the biggest responsibilities both you and your puppy's breeder have, and can have the greatest positive influence on your dog's personality than almost anything else you can do.

What's the Best Age to Socialize My Puppy?

The sensitive period for socialization occurs between four and twelve weeks of age. The word "sensitive" means that attachments and acceptance of unfamiliar things develop almost effortlessly between these ages.

During the sensitive period, most puppies are like little sponges, soaking up new experiences. They are willing to try new things and accept people and other animals readily. This is what makes socialization so easy–puppies aren't afraid of much, and they enjoy bouncing from one new experience to another.

The Breeder's Responsibilities. Because the sensitive period begins when puppies are still with mom and littermates, breeders have the significant responsibility of starting the socialization process. A litter of puppies should be part of the household. They shouldn't be housed in a dog run, a barn, garage, or any other type of out building.

By being housed in the living environment, puppies become accustomed to normal household sounds from birth. Noises from the dishwasher, furnace, vacuum cleaner, telephone, as well as everyday conversation and the hustle and bustle of a family's day-to-day activities are all the "background noise" of the puppy's life. These experiences get your puppy's socialization period off to a good start so those first critical weeks aren't wasted.

Your puppy's breeder should also have made a point to gently handle and spend individual social time with your puppy and her littermates every day. At six to eight weeks, your puppy should have been introduced to people other than the breeder's family, and weather permitting, even had a few brief outings to the great outdoors in a nonpublic place.

If you acquired your puppy from a shelter or rescue group. Puppies from these sources can become wonderful companions. However, try to find out as much as you can about a puppy's early experiences before you adopt. Puppies born to feral dogs, puppies rescued from neglected or abusive environments, and puppies that for any reason–including irresponsible breeders–didn't have opportunities to have pleasant experiences with a variety of people from six weeks of age on are more likely to grow up being fearful or defensive. Read more about the consequences of a lack of socialization later in this book.

Now It's Your Turn. Now that your puppy is in your care, it's your turn to do everything in your power to help her reach her full potential and become a behaviorally healthy adult. Puppy classes provide excellent socialization experiences. But don't stop there.

Follow the suggestions for socialization experiences later in this section, and make up others that might be especially important for your puppy, given the sort of activities you want her to be able to do as an adult.

How and to What Should I Socialize My Puppy?

Let's answer the "how" question first. Socialization experiences should be fun for your puppy. Her new experiences should be paired with treats, gentle petting, or chances to play. If she seems a bit nervous about something new, don't force her to approach the new item, person or animal. Take it slow, creating baby steps for her.

If she's afraid to approach a tall man with a beard, ask the man to sit down so he doesn't look as frightening. If your puppy runs from the vacuum cleaner, put it in another room at first when you turn it on. Find ways to make scary situations less so for your puppy, so that she can overcome her fear.

What kinds of socialization experiences do puppies need? Consider what your puppy will be doing as an adult. Do you want her to enjoy traveling in the car with you? Then you'll need to start acclimating her to car rides now.

You'll obviously want your puppy to be good with friendly, well-behaved children, so now is the time to socialize her to kids. This is especially true if you don't have children, but know you will in the future. If your dog is two or three years old when you start your family and she's had little to no experience with children, she is likely to have problems when your baby starts to crawl and walk.

Make sure your puppy is socialized to other dogs, cats, and people of all different shapes, sizes and ages. Expose her to tall, big men with deep rumbling voices, and short, small women with squeaky voices. Men with beards, hats and glasses. Let her meet people who walk with a limp or a cane, and people in unusual dress such as big coats, floppy hats, sunglasses or uniforms. For a few weeks, have every person your puppy meets, both at and away from your home, give her a treat.

Gradually expose your puppy to noisy objects such as hair dryers, vacuum cleaners, furnaces, washers and dryers, and lawnmowers. Don't forget quickly moving objects such as bicycles, people on skateboards and roller skates, joggers, automobiles and delivery trucks.

Give your puppy the chance to experience many different environments such as soccer games at the park, a backyard barbecue or a visit to friends in the city or the suburbs. Take your puppy wading in the lake. Let your puppy walk on grass, concrete, rocks, dirt, and teach her to climb stairs.

Take your puppy for visits to the veterinary hospital and the groomer. Because scary things often happen to your puppy at these facilities, the socialization visits should be just for petting and getting treats.

If you want to crate train your puppy, doing so now will be much easier than getting her used to a crate when she is an adult. Refer to the crate training procedures in this book.

You want your puppy to have a good time experiencing all these new and intriguing events. That's what socialization is all about–your puppy learning that the world is a fun place, not a scary one.

Until your puppy has completed her series of vaccinations, be cautious about taking her places where she could be exposed to contagious diseases from other dogs. Follow your veterinarian's recommendations, but don't isolate your puppy so much that she doesn't get the socialization experiences she so critically needs at these ages. Puppy classes provide great experiences to get started socializing your puppy.

What Happens if I Don't Socialize My Puppy?

Without good socialization, your puppy will not grow into the confident, friendly dog and the enjoyable companion you dreamed of. If your puppy led a reclusive early life or had a rough beginning for other reasons, you may already have noticed the effects on her behavior. She may be fearful, anxious, or act like she has a chip on her shoulder.

Lost opportunities during puppyhood can never be regained. Later in life, it is very difficult to "rehabilitate" puppies who were not well socialized. Poorly socialized puppies don't develop good social skills, and are uncomfortable in new situations. Poorly socialized puppies often act as though they were abused, because they are afraid of harmless things, and they seem not to be able to remember, or generalize their later, positive experiences.

A dog that is afraid of men, and finally learns to accept Uncle Joe, doesn't readily generalize this acceptance to Uncle Pete. Learning that one or two men are OK doesn't generalize to males in general. This generalization occurs easily during the sensitive period.

What Should I Do about My Fearful Puppy?

Whenever your puppy acts afraid, make the event easier, and less threatening for her. For example, ask a person greeting your puppy to step back a few steps, sit on the floor, or not look directly at your puppy.

Muffle a noise that is bothering your puppy, or move it farther away. Pair the noise or the person with something your puppy likes–a tidbit, a toy, a relaxing massage.

Try not to overwhelm your puppy by taking her someplace like a fireworks display, or a boisterous Super Bowl party. Give some thought to your puppy's personality and what you think she is ready to handle. Take baby steps, not giant leaps.

Fear Phases Occur During the Socialization Period

Your puppy has two fear periods you must know about so you can be somewhat protective of your puppy at these times. At eight weeks of age, and again at twelve weeks, your puppy may show a distinct reluctance to do activities she's done before, or approach anything new.

At Eight Weeks. During the eighth week, give your puppy normal experiences, but don't allow her to be traumatized. This is not a good age to adopt your puppy, or to allow her to be frightened by a visit to the veterinarian, rambunctious children, etc.

Puppies can take a long time to recover from frightening experiences at this age. By nine weeks, most puppies return to more characteristic, outgoing patterns.

At Twelve Weeks. Twelve weeks signals the close of the sensitive socialization period. Increasing fear of the unfamiliar is what causes this period to end. You may notice a more permanent change in your puppy's acceptance of new things. She may not approach strangers with the reckless abandon she did when younger. Continue her socialization, but recognize that your puppy's acceptance of new things may take longer.

 ## When Can I Stop Socializing My Puppy?

The short answer is never. It's unrealistic to expect puppyhood socialization experiences to last a lifetime. After the socialization period ends at three months, don't make the mistake of isolating your puppy in the backyard, and not giving her opportunities to continue meeting new people, experiencing new environments, and playing with other dogs.

Even if you acquired your puppy when she was older, start socializing her right away. You may have to work harder to do this, as older, poorly socialized puppies are more cautious about things they haven't seen before. Use lots of irresistible tidbits, favorite toys, and relaxing touch to encourage your older puppy to take on the world, a tiny bit at time.

Continued socialization is particularly important through two years of age. Adult patterns of aggressive behavior appear during this adolescent stage, so your young adult must learn how to get along with other dogs, grown-up to grown-up.

Chapter 4
Understanding Dominance and
Your Puppy's Role in the Family

Almost all of us have heard about dominance problems in dogs. These are most often described as situations where dogs become threatening or aggressive to their owners. Some people have argued that doing certain "dominance exercises" with young puppies can prevent aggression and other behavior problems. Is this true? Exactly what is dominance in dogs? Are dominance exercises necessary to prevent behavior problems in dogs?

 ## What is Dominance?

In their relationships, dogs will inevitably compete with each other over food, treats, toys, special resting or sleeping places, attention from people, and which one goes through the door first. To establish which animal gets first access to things dogs think are important, they usually establish social hierarchies, or so-called dominance relationships.

These relationships, and the roles each dog assumes within them, allow dogs to work out competitive situations without fighting. Threats, appeasement (submission), deference and avoidance are often substituted for aggression. The "dominant dog" (more precisely—the dog in the dominant role) isn't always the most aggressive dog. A dominant dog can get his way without being aggressive.

The dog in a dominant role in a relationship gets what he wants by a look or a subtle threat or because the subordinate dogs simply move away. Establishing roles help dogs sort out the "rules" for their relationship, and who can do what to whom. In stable groups of dogs, there is very little threatening or fighting because each dog has learned the social rules of their relationships.

However, dominance relationships among dogs aren't always simple. There may not be one "dominant dog" in a relationship. Who gets what first may depend on the situation. One dog may get access to the food first while another is able to get attention from the owners first.

Which dog assumes the dominant role will also depend on the social partner. Dog A may be able to take away toys from Dog B, but not from Dog C.

How Do Dogs Relate to People?

When dogs live with people they tend to treat people like they are dogs and include them in their dominance relationships. However, dogs almost always defer to people. Dogs just seem to automatically think of people as higher ranking than themselves and usually will give way to whatever people want.

Thousands of years of domestication have developed a tendency for dogs to be submissive to us. It is rare for a dog, and even more rare for a puppy, to dominantly challenge anyone in the household in which he lives. Confusion about what dominance is and how it relates to the person-dog relationship has led to a number of misconceptions about dominance and behavior problems in dogs. Here are some of them.

Misconceptions about Dominance and Dog Behavior Problems

1. *Dogs are "status seekers" and are always looking for ways to be in control and be "the boss." If you don't put your puppy in his place, bad things will happen.*
   Puppies may try to get their way but it's not because they are trying to be dominant. Your puppy just naturally will try different behaviors and different strategies to see what works to get what he wants, and to see whether listening to you is important. Your job is to show your puppy that the behaviors you want are also the ones that get him what he wants.

2. *Dogs become destructive, housesoil, bark, howl and escape because the owners are not dominant over them.*
   These behaviors have any number of motivations, none of which have to do with dominance. Behaviors that relate to social dominance involve competition and social communication. Puppies are destructive because they are curious, they housesoil because they aren't yet housetrained, and they may vocalize because they are afraid or lonely.

3. *Dogs that are disobedient or slow to obey their owners do so because the owners are not dominant over them.*
   Social dominance is not the same thing as being obedient. Your puppy may not sit when you tell him because he is distracted, confused about what he is supposed to do, or because your training is incomplete. Whether or not your puppy does what you tell him to do may have nothing to do with whether you are in the dominant role in the relationship. This is an extremely important distinction and a major source of confusion in the popular literature on dogs.

4. *Dogs that are aggressive to the family, to unfamiliar people or to other dogs do so because the owners are not dominant over them.*
   It's more likely that these problems stem from fear rather than dominance. Rarely a puppy, or more often, an adult dog may use aggression to get his way with family members or with other dogs. This is a very serious problem. If your puppy is showing his teeth, growling or otherwise threatening you, a very serious problem may be developing and you should talk with your veterinarian or local animal shelter immediately about a referral to a certified behaviorist or trainer.

5. *Dominance exercises such as alpha roll over or scruff-shake must be done to prevent dogs from becoming dominant over their owners.*
   These procedures are not beneficial. In fact, if they are conducted in a harsh, intimidating manner they can actually create fearful and defensive problems. Contrary to popular belief, these exercises do **not** mimic dog behavior. Both you and your puppy are better off without them.

6. *Puppy tests can reliably predict which puppies will become dominant as adults.*
   Research has shown that puppy tests cannot reliably predict behavior problems including dominance problems. Dogs develop behavior problems for many, many reasons. Learning and experience have such great influences on your puppy's behavior, that it's really silly to think that one simple response can be predictive of something as complex as social relationships.

It is not necessary to feed your puppy after you eat, to be the one to start and end play time, or not allow your puppy to sleep on the bed or furniture to let your puppy know that you are in the dominant role.

If you focus too much on dominance you may end up not with a loving relationship with your dog but with a dog that is fearful and doesn't trust you. You may create even more behavior problems for him.

Your relationship with your dog is complex, with lots of give and take, and includes affection as well as occasional conflicts.

A better way to think about your relationship with your puppy is as a parent to a child. As with your children, you need to set limits on your puppy's behavior, train him, provide good care and a loving, predictable, and safe environment.

You don't need to use "alpha rolls," scruff shakes, strong physical punishment or confrontational methods in dealing with your children, and you don't need them with your puppy.

You may need to communicate differently with your puppy than with your children but the goals are the same. Think about how you can be a good parent for your puppy rather than being the "alpha." You can use our Five-Step Positive Proaction Plan to establish this kind of relationship.

 ## Help Your Puppy Do the Right Thing

Make it pleasant for your puppy to give in to you and to do what you want him to do. Use treats, play and other rewards to encourage your puppy to do what you want. You don't need to have confrontations with your puppy.

On a regular basis, practice taking food, treats, toys and objects your puppy may "steal" away from your puppy. Use tasty treats or other rewards to make it worth his while to give up what he has. Refer to the section on teaching "give" for details.

Work on the handling, nail trimming and brushing exercises described in this book. Doing these exercises in a pleasant way teaches your puppy to enjoy the procedures, rather than responding with fear or aggression.

46

Raising a Behaviorally Healthy Puppy

Keep Bad Habits from Developing

If your puppy doesn't like to have his feet touched, to be picked up, to have his food or toys taken away, don't ignore these problems. Use the procedures described throughout this book to teach your puppy to enjoy these events. If you allow your puppy to decide he won't tolerate these procedures, you are setting a dangerous precedent.

Be good about following through with what you ask your puppy to do. You don't need to be gruff or mean, just persistent. If you tell your puppy to sit, keep working with him until he does. Refer to later sections in this book on how to teach basic behaviors such as sit, down and stay.

If your puppy threatens you or others, seek professional help immediately. The longer you wait to seek help, the stronger the habit will become.

 ## Meet Your Puppy's Behavioral and Developmental Needs

Puppies need play, exercise and social time with the family. Your puppy needs to be part of a social group–your family–not isolated in the backyard or home alone for most of her formative months.

Puppies need lots of feedback from you to make it easy for them to learn what you like. When your puppy doesn't struggle when you wipe his feet, doesn't protest when you take away a chewie, or walk by his bed, reward him with a tidbit and a pet.

 ## Use the "Take-Away" Method to Discourage Behaviors You Don't Like

If your puppy plays too roughly, or paws or nips for attention, walk away from him, and end the encounter. Don't encourage this behavior and don't get into a confrontation with him. Follow the advice on how to use the take-away method given in other sections of this book.

Make Discipline the Last Resort and Use it Correctly

Alpha rolls, scruff shaking and other kinds of confrontational methods are not necessary to develop a good relationship with your puppy. They can actually cause fear and aggression problems.

Even if your puppy is showing threatening behavior by growling or baring his teeth, physical or corporal punishment such as hitting, swatting or spanking should NEVER be used. These behaviors are more likely to be motivated by fear and defensiveness rather than dominance problems.

Talk first to your veterinarian to be sure there isn't a medical reason for this behavior. Then ask your veterinarian for a referral to a certified behaviorist or trainer.

Chapter 5
A Step-by-Step Guide to Crate Training

Sometimes it is necessary to use a crate, or to confine your dog in a small area to help house train her, to help prevent destruction, or to manage other behaviors. Crate training is easy, but it does take time and patience on your part. If you do it correctly, your dog will be comfortable in her crate and go in willingly whenever you ask her.

The idea that dogs are "a denning species" is often misunderstood. Wild canids and dogs use a den to give birth to and raise puppies. Adult dogs are not predisposed to spending long periods of time in small spaces by themselves. They have to be gradually habituated and trained to accept these conditions. Puppies are never alone in a den, but are frequently by themselves when crated.

These crate training procedures can also be used to teach your puppy to be comfortable while confined in other small areas such as a laundry room, mud room, bathroom or kitchen. If you are going to use these areas for confinement, be sure to puppy-proof them and put papers or puppy pads down for your puppy to relieve herself on if she will be confined beyond her need for a potty break.

Remember these important points:

- Your puppy must be comfortable and relaxed at each step before progressing to the next.
- The most common mistake you can make is trying to do too much too soon.
- Do NOT attempt to leave your puppy alone in the crate without progressing through the following steps.

 Help Your Puppy Do the Right Thing

Goal #1: Your Puppy Enters the Crate Willingly

How to do: Toss treats and toys inside and let your puppy's natural curiosity encourage her to explore the crate, or feed your puppy meals in the crate for a day or so. Be sure to tie the door back so it doesn't accidentally slam shut and frighten your puppy.

How long should it take: Most puppies can accomplish this step the first day. Fearful puppies may require several days of training.

Goal #2: Your Puppy Can Be Relaxed in the Crate with You in Sight for 15-20 Minutes

How to do: Tell your puppy to "kennel up," and give your puppy a special toy. This special toy should be available only when your puppy is crated and will help her look forward to being crated. We recommend any of the safe chew toys that can be filled with goodies discussed in Chapter 8 on chewing behavior. As your puppy settles and chews on her toy, close the crate door for just a few seconds. Stay close by, where your puppy can see you and you can observe her behavior. Open the door and let your puppy out, but don't fuss over her. Be sure to pick up the special toy, or leave it in the crate and shut the door.

If your puppy was calm, repeat after a few minutes, and leave her in the crate a few minutes longer. Don't overdo these repetitions. Give your puppy plenty of free time in between. Gradually increase your puppy's time in the crate until you reach your goal of 20 minutes. This step could be easily practiced while watching TV, or during part of your mealtime, as long as the crate is kept near you. Don't forget the "kennel up" command and your puppy's special toy.

How long should it take: Most puppies can accomplish this step within one to three days. If your puppy has been previously traumatized or is very fearful, this step could require a week or more.

Goal #3: Your Puppy Can Relax in the Crate for 30 Minutes with You Out of Sight or Overnight

How to do: Begin by crating your puppy for less than 20 minutes while you are doing other things, such as chores around the house. At first, so your puppy knows you are still nearby, come back into the room frequently, but ignore her, and then walk away again. Slowly increase the portion of out of sight time until it's up to the full 20 minutes. Work on the last 10 minutes the same way—in and out of her sight until you reach 30 minutes. At this point, you can also try crating your puppy overnight, but the crate should be moved to your bedroom for this part of your puppy's training.

How long should it take: Most puppies can accomplish this step in two to four days. Fearful puppies or those with previous bad experiences could require a week or even two. Some puppies will sleep in a crate overnight from day one, as long as the crate is next to your bed.

Goal #4: Your Puppy Can Stay in the Crate for an Hour When You are Gone

How to do: With very little fanfare, crate your puppy using the "kennel up" words and the special toy. ***Be sure to take your puppy's collar off to prevent any injuries.*** Calmly leave the house and return within 30 minutes. It's a good idea to video or audio tape your puppy to be sure she remains calm and relaxed. Over the next day or two, crate your puppy when you leave the house for increasingly longer time periods. However, continue to do some very brief crating times both when you are home and away so that your puppy doesn't think that crating times are always becoming longer and always mean she will be alone.

How long should it take: Most puppies can accomplish this step in three to four days. If your puppy has had problems, this could require as much as two to four weeks.

By now, you should be able to leave your puppy crated when you are gone from the house for several hours.

 ## Keep Bad Habits from Developing

You must be sure your puppy does not become fearful or panicked in her crate. You can assess this by looking for the following:

◆ Reluctance to enter the crate
◆ Excessive whining, barking or other vocalizing

- ◆ Attempts to get out of the crate
- ◆ Soiling in the crate, even if crated for brief time periods
- ◆ Finding your puppy's fur wet from saliva when you return home
- ◆ Evidence your puppy has been so frantic that she has moved the crate
- ◆ Any damage to the crate, or injuries to your puppy, from escape attempts

If you notice any of these signs, the first thing to do is to backtrack several steps in the crate training process. You may have tried to do too much too soon. Give your puppy additional easier experiences with the crate–shorter times with you close by. A sample of crate training times you could try might be–5 minutes, 2 minutes, 10 minutes, 20 minutes, 7 minutes, 25 minutes, 45 minutes, 15 minutes, etc.

Perhaps you need to give your puppy a more enjoyable toy when she's crated. Go back to not closing the door if necessary.

Be patient with the training and your puppy. A little extra work now will pay off well in the future. If you still have problems, talk to your veterinarian first, who may decide to refer you to a certified behaviorist or trainer.

 ## Meet Your Puppy's Behavioral and Developmental Needs

Be careful to not overdo the amount of time your puppy spends in the crate. Be sure to give her enough "potty breaks" and check to see she is not becoming fearful. A crate is meant to be a short-term training and management tool, and not a place where your puppy spends most of her time. Your puppy needs plenty of exercise, play, and social time with you. Balance your puppy's need to learn to be comfortable and confined when alone, with the important socialization requirements.

 ## Make Discipline the Last Resort and Use it Correctly

Crate training doesn't require discipline or punishment. See the list of FAQ's if your puppy is barking, whining or chewing up her bedding.

Frequently Asked Questions about Crates and Crate Training

1. How do I choose the right crate for my puppy?

Your puppy should be able to stand up easily, turn around with no effort and lie down comfortably.

There are predominantly two different styles of crates–molded plastic and wire crates. Plastic crates tend to be better suited for travel, are fairly lightweight, provide more insulation and can be split in half. When split in half, the bottom half can be used as a puppy bed.

Wire crates offer your puppy a better view, more air circulation, and can be easily folded and stored under a bed or in a closet. Both plastic and wire have advantages and disadvantages and your decision will be based on your individual needs. We usually don't recommend soft-sided cloth crates for puppies because of the likelihood puppies will chew on them.

2. How should I prepare my puppy's new crate?

The key is to help your puppy be comfortable. Place a towel or blanket in the crate to provide a soft surface to lie on. If your puppy tears up these items, try substituting soft rubber matting, obtainable through pet stores or catalogs. Don't forget your puppy's special toy.

3. Where's the best place in my home for my crate?

Place the crate where the family spends a lot of time. A family room, living room or kitchen are good spots. Avoid basements or other areas where the family does not spend much time.

You do not want your puppy to feel isolated during the crate training process. This could cause immediate problems. Remember that you may be moving your puppy's crate from its daytime location to the bedroom during initial overnight crating.

4. Why should I crate train my puppy?

If you aren't familiar with a crate, you may feel as though you are putting your puppy in a cage. But when used properly, a crate is instead a safe place for your puppy when you can't be there to supervise. A crate makes a useful behavior management tool.

A crate will help keep your puppy safe from household hazards when you're not around and will also help limit her destructive behavior.

A crate is a great way to transport your puppy and can also be an essential tool in housetraining. Keep in mind that a crate is not meant to be a full time "nanny" and it does not replace good training and puppy raising skills.

5. Why go through this crate training process? Can't I just put my puppy in the crate and leave?

Having your puppy accept the crate requires a step-by-step training process. At first, the crate is unfamiliar to your puppy, and being confined there without an introduction process would be distressing.

Once your puppy has a bad experience with crating, it is much more difficult, and sometimes impossible, to teach her that the crate is a safe place. You don't want your puppy to panic and hurt herself trying to get out of the crate because she isn't used to it. Crate training will make things better for your puppy and for you.

6. How will a crate help in housetraining my puppy?

The value of crating is that it prevents your puppy from having the chance to make a mistake and soil in the house when you can't supervise her. She will be reluctant to soil her sleeping area, as long as she isn't frightened and isn't crated too long.

7. How can I use a crate to limit my puppy's destructive behavior?

When you're not around to supervise your puppy, crating her will prevent her from having the chance to find things to chew on that she shouldn't. See Chapter 8: Have Shoe, Will Chew.

8. What if my puppy soils in the crate?

Something is wrong. Maybe your puppy didn't completely relieve herself before being crated. Next time, make sure she does so. Did you crate your puppy for longer than she could control herself? Refer to the housetraining section in this book.

Your puppy may be frightened or anxious when crated. Is your puppy showing other warning signs from the list above? You must determine why she is frightened.

Is your puppy afraid of noises such as thunder or trash trucks? You may need help desensitizing or socializing your puppy.

Is your puppy afraid of being left alone? Puppies need time to adjust to being away from their mom and littermates. If you puppy seems panicky when left alone, she may not do well in a crate until she has had more time to adjust. Begin by leaving her confined in a room by herself with a baby gate while you are in another part of the house for short time periods.

Any number of medical conditions could make your puppy need to relieve herself more often. Have your puppy checked by your veterinarian. If you still have problems, your veterinarian can refer you to a certified behaviorist or trainer.

9. What if my puppy whines or barks to get out of the crate?
You can ignore mild vocalizations. When your puppy is quiet, either let her out of the crate or reward her with a tidbit or a pet. If she sounds really upset or panicked, either let her out of the crate or sit nearby, put your hand into the crate and talk quietly to your puppy. It's better to help your puppy calm down rather than forcing her to stay crated and become more agitated until she begins to fear the crate.

Determine why your puppy became so upset. Have you moved too fast through the crate training process? Go back a few steps in the process. Are other things upsetting her, as discussed previously? If your puppy is vocalizing persistently and/or intensely, talk to your veterinarian who can refer you to a certified behaviorist or trainer.

10. Will my puppy ever grow out of needing to be crated?
Yes. A puppy should be fully housetrained and should show no signs of destructive behaviors when you are home before you try leaving her alone free in the house. Your puppy could be anywhere from six months to two years old before she can be trusted alone out of the crate.

Puppy-proofed mud rooms or laundry rooms can be used to make the transition to being crated. Gradually let your puppy spend more time in the transition area or free in the house when you are gone over a period of days or weeks. Watch for housesoiling, destructiveness and signs of fear or distress. If you see any of these, go back to shorter times out of the crate and then gradually lengthen them as your puppy adapts to her new freedom without supervision.

Many people never leave their dogs completely free in the house when alone, but rather, restrict their dog's access to certain areas that have been puppy proofed and that are easy to clean, such as a family room, kitchen or mud room. Whether or not you let your dog have free run of your house or restrict her to some degree will depend upon your family's needs and her behavior.

11. Will some puppies never quite adjust to a crate?
As long as your puppy never has a bad experience with the crate, you should be able to crate train her. There is the rare puppy who, for whatever reason, seems to have a problem with confinement of any kind. If you need help, talk to your veterinarian first, who can refer you to a certified behaviorist or trainer.

Chapter 6
Housetraining Your Puppy

Probably more has been written about housetraining dogs than almost any other behavioral topic. There are even entire books about it, such as How To Housebreak Your Dog In Five Days. Because so much information is available, you have undoubtedly run across some myths and misconceptions about housetraining, although you may not have recognized them as such.

If you remember nothing else about housetraining remember this–your goal is NOT to teach your puppy where **not** to relieve himself, your goal is to teach you puppy **where you want him to go!** Housetraining a dog or puppy is not rocket science, but does require attention to detail and strict consistency.

 ## Housetraining, not House*breaking*

Please notice that we call this section *housetraining*. It is a *training* process–therefore we talk about *housetraining,* **NOT** *housebreaking.* This may seem like a small detail but it really reflects an important attitude. You are **training** your puppy to do what you want, not trying to break him of a bad habit. Puppies don't come with bad habits, only natural behaviors.

As with other aspects of behavior wellness, housetraining involves teaching your dog where **to go,** rather than scolding him for not going in the correct place. *Housetraining need not require discipline or punishment.* We easily housetrained our puppy Coral, who is on the cover, without even using the word "no" or any other type of discipline. Years ago, the recommended discipline for soiling in the house was to swat the puppy on the rear with a rolled up newspaper. Scientific advances have provided a better use for the rolled up newspaper. If your puppy soils the house, take the newspaper and whack yourself on the side of the head while repeating, "I should have been watching my puppy," ten times!

Basis for Housetraining

Three objectives form the basis for housetraining: 1. Help your puppy develop habits or preferences for where (location), and on what (surface or texture) he likes to eliminate; 2. Make use of your puppy's natural tendency to relieve himself away from his living areas, where he rests, sleeps, plays and eats; and 3. Develop a mutual communication system so your puppy can signal you when he needs to go outside.

If you follow the housetraining procedures listed below, you should be able to successfully housetrain your puppy with a minimum number of "accidents." Accidents usually reflect a breakdown in one of these procedures, and require the use of the rolled up newspaper described before! Housetraining procedures are organized around three parts of our Five-Step Positive Proactive Plan for a Behaviorally Healthy Dog.

 ## Help Your Puppy Do the Right Thing

Put Your Puppy on a Regular Feeding Schedule
While it may be convenient for you to have food available for your puppy all the time, this has a number of drawbacks. If your puppy eats at irregular times, you will have a difficult time predicting when he needs to relieve himself. Establishing regular feeding times also makes the tidbit rewards you will be using more motivating because your dog will be hungrier in between meals. Not having food out all the time also minimizes your puppy's opportunities to guard his food, and doesn't provide a temptation to crawling babies or toddlers.

Always Use Consistent Cue Words or Phrases
There are two kinds of cues—one to encourage your dog to go outside and the other to trigger elimination behavior. "Do you want to go outside?" is an example of the first, and "Go potty" is an example of the second. The "outside" cue should be given as you are walking toward the door to let your puppy out or put his leash on, and the "potty" cue should be repeated in the elimination location until your puppy begins

to relieve himself. At that point, begin praising him, and when he is finished, pet him and offer a tidbit as well. Be consistent with your praise.

Learn Your Puppy's Signals and Respond Immediately

Puppies usually start sniffing and circling before they eliminate. Be on the alert for these behaviors and immediately take your puppy outside. Your puppy may have unique signals that you'll learn to recognize. At first, don't expect your puppy to go to the door to let you know he needs to go. Your puppy must first learn where to relieve himself, second how to get there (by following you) and finally how to communicate to you to let him out. This will take time. In the meantime, you must respond to the signals your puppy is giving you that mean he's getting ready to relieve himself.

 ## Keep Bad Habits from Developing

Supervision to Minimize Mistakes is Crucial

Because a major part of housetraining is getting your puppy in the habit of going where you want him to, you simply cannot allow bad habits to develop. If your puppy goes inside often enough, he will quickly connect these inside locations with relieving himself, rather than with the outside location you want him to prefer.

Until your puppy is reliably letting you know when he needs to go outside, he must always be in sight. When you can't watch him, he must be confined in an area, such as a kitchen, or exercise pen where you can paper train him, or in a crate, so he doesn't have the chance to soil in the house. You cannot crate your puppy for longer than he can control his bladder and bowels. (Refer to the section on crate training for more information.)

Clean Any Soiled Areas with a Good Enzymatic Cleaner Designed for Pets

Odors from previous soiling can attract your puppy back to those areas, so it is crucial that you thoroughly neutralize these odors. Enzymatic cleaners, or those with genetically engineered bacteria, degrade or break up the waste products, thereby eliminating any odors. Household cleaners or vinegar do not do this, and only mask the odor. Clean up soiled areas as soon as possible to minimize how much the material soaks into the carpet and pad. We recommend a product with a laughable name– Anti-Icky-Poo®. Despite its humorous name, it gives great results. Purchase it from our Web site at www.AnimalBehaviorAssociates.com or see the Order Form at the back of the book.

Meet Your Puppy's Behavioral and Developmental Needs

Take Your Puppy Outside at Predictable Times to Relieve Himself
During housetraining, give your puppy the chance to relieve himself as soon as he wakes up (in the morning or from a nap), within 20 minutes after he eats, and after he's been playing excitedly for a time. In between these times, he should be taken outside frequently, at intervals appropriate for his age. Very young puppies (8-10 weeks) may need to relieve themselves every hour or two. Older puppies may be able to control themselves for three or four hours.

Provide a Sufficient Number of "Potty Breaks" Throughout the Day
If you are away from home for long hours, you must either paper train your puppy, or have someone come to give him a potty break. Puppies cannot go for an eight-hour workday without a chance to relieve themselves. Consider a pet sitting service, a dog door, or hiring a neighbor to come in and let your puppy outside for a brief "potty walk."

Adult, housetrained dogs can probably last five to six hours before needing a "potty break." Much depends on their age, health status, activity level, time of day, and the timing of their food and water intake. While some dogs are able to go eight to ten hours without eliminating when left home alone, this is probably uncomfortable for them. Try to avoid it if possible. Their ability to go overnight without eliminating does not necessarily apply to daytime, because of the factors listed above.

If you have no choice but to provide an indoor potty area, use puppy training pads, not newspaper.

Provide Dog-Friendly Locations for Elimination and Accustom Your Puppy to Accepting a Variety of Surfaces

We don't understand all of the factors that influence the locations dogs prefer for elimination. However, early experience seems to play an important role.

It is important that you accustom your puppy to the types of locations he'll most likely be using throughout life. If your city puppy will need to eliminate on cement, gravel or other hard surfaces, accustom him to them now. It is probably a good idea to get your puppy to accept a number of different types of surfaces for elimination.

 ### Make Discipline the Last Resort and Use it Correctly

Housetraining can be accomplished without punishment by following the procedures described here. **NEVER** rub your puppy's nose in his urine or feces and **NEVER** hit him.

If you catch your puppy eliminating in the house, quickly get him to follow you outside, or pick him up if necessary. Do this in an encouraging, not a threatening, manner, otherwise he will likely run from you, be afraid to go outside or be afraid to relieve himself in front of you.

If you find a "mess" after the fact, clean it up and do nothing to your puppy. **NEVER** try to show your puppy the mess and discipline him, as you will confuse him and create more problems.

Chapter 7
Helping Your Puppy Get Along with Your Other Pets

You've likely already done the initial introductions between your puppy and your other pets. Things may be going smoothly, or you may have already encountered a few bumps in the road.

There are a variety of steps you can take to smooth things out, and help your other pets work out a good relationship with your puppy.

If You Have Other Dogs

The most common reason adult dogs get grumpy with puppies is because puppies don't yet know what rules to follow in the relationship.

Puppies are rambunctious, energetic and playful. Your puppy may jump on your older dog, chew on his ears and pester him. If your adult dog takes exception to this, he may snap, growl or snarl at your puppy.

These are perfectly normal and acceptable forms of canine communication, as long as your older dog doesn't take them to extremes. Your adult dog needs to have some way of setting limits with your puppy and telling her when enough is enough.

These communicative behaviors may startle or frighten your puppy but won't hurt her. If your adult dog is actually biting your puppy to the point of injury, a more serious problem exists and you should talk with your veterinarian about a referral to a certified behaviorist or trainer immediately. Do not let this go, and assume it will get better. You will be risking your puppy's safety.

You can prevent many problems by using our Five-Step Positive Proaction Plan to help your puppy and your other dogs develop good relationships.

Help Your Puppy and Your Adult Dog Do the Right Thing

If you are petting your older dog and your puppy approaches, make this a fun event, rather than a competition. "Jolly" your adult dog as your puppy runs up.

Start teaching your puppy to sit before you pet her, so that she doesn't rush up and crash into your adult dog in her excitement. If you are petting your adult dog with your right hand, use your left hand to encourage your puppy to approach from that side, creating a bit of social distance between the two.

 ## Keep Bad Habits from Developing

Until you are sure your puppy is safe with your adult dog, supervise them constantly, and do not leave them alone together. Your puppy is a baby, and your adult dog could inadvertently hurt her just by playing too rough. Because your puppy will most likely be crated when left alone, this won't be a concern. If necessary however, use baby gates to create separate areas of the house where your dog and puppy can still see one another but are physically separated. Putting your puppy in an exercise pen or puppy playpen during the initial introduction and when left alone is another option.

 ## Meet Your Puppy's Behavioral and Developmental Needs

It's not your adult dog's job to be your puppy's personal playmate. While the two of them may enjoy playing together, your puppy's need for play and activity may far exceed that of your older dog.

To take the burden off of your other dog(s), you must make time to play with and exercise your puppy. Your older dog may also need some quiet time away from the nonstop pace of your puppy.

You may want to put your dog in a favorite out of the way spot, such as your bedroom or a family room, so she isn't bothered when your puppy is running laps around the living room.

Meet Your Resident Dog's Behavioral and Developmental Needs

Your resident dog will be less upset if the routines he's accustomed to don't change. Try to feed him in the same place you always have, let him sleep in his usual place, and walk him on the same schedule.

It's easy to pay more attention to your puppy than to your adult dog. Be careful to avoid this pitfall. Spend quality, individual time with your adult dog when your puppy is napping.

Your puppy will undoubtedly want to share your older dog's toys, so you may need to provide the same toy for each dog–plus one. If a tennis ball is the toy of choice, and you have two dogs, make sure you have at least three tennis balls.

 ## Use the "Take-Away" Method to Discourage Behaviors You Don't Like

If you are petting your adult dog, your puppy approaches, and your adult growls, stop petting her and walk away. You want to teach your older dog that she can't prevent you from petting your puppy. If she wants continued attention from you, she must accept the puppy's presence.

If play between your puppy and your adult dog gets too rough or out of control, interrupt the play session and get each interested in another activity. While your adult dog should be allowed to set reasonable limits for your puppy, at the same time she shouldn't be allowed to "bully" your puppy either. If she does, put your dog in time-out for three to five minutes. Choose a location your dog doesn't want to be, such as a mud room or laundry room, where there isn't anything fun to do.

 ## Make Discipline the Last Resort and Use it Correctly

It's risky to use aversive techniques in response to problem behaviors from your adult dog toward your puppy. If through this process your dog learns to associate "bad things" with your puppy's presence, you have made things worse, not better. If the "take-away" method hasn't worked, you might try _calmly_ squirting your dog with a fine stream of water to interrupt "bullying" or out of control play. If this isn't effective after a few applications, you may need professional help for your pets.

If your dog is having problems with your puppy, some sort of emotional arousal–fear, frustration, anger–is already present. Yelling at or hitting your dog only increases this arousal. If you are resorting to these techniques, it may be because you don't know how else to handle the developing problems. In that case, talk to your veterinarian about a referral to a certified behaviorist or trainer who can give you other options.

 ## Your Resident Dog May Not Be "Dominant"

Initially, it's likely your puppy will acquiesce, or give in to your adult dog when it comes to who will control the toys, space on the couch, etc. But as your puppy gets just a little older and settles into your home, don't be surprised if she decides to test the status-quo.

In general, it's best if you let your dogs sort things out without interference from you. The exception to this would be if either dog is being injured during conflicts that arise, or one dog is being an unreasonable bully. For example, if your adult dog tries to guard all the toys and never wants your puppy to play with anything, you need to find professional assistance.

Whether your puppy or your older dog will ultimately assume a dominant role in their relationship depends on their individual characteristics. Just because your resident dog was there first, and is older or larger doesn't automatically confer a higher social rank.

 ## If You have Cats

Most puppies just want to play with and chase cats, not hurt them. However, most cats are not thrilled about this idea. If your cat is the confident, outgoing type, he may quite easily set his own limits with your puppy with some timely hisses and swats. Even if your cat is declawed, he can still successfully intimidate your puppy. If your puppy backs off and respects your cat's personal space, the two will likely develop a workable relationship. Use the Five-Step Positive Proaction Plan to help your puppy and your cat learn to respect each other.

 ## Help Your Puppy and Your Cat Do the Right Thing

Set up practice sessions with your cat and your puppy. Try placing each animal on either side of a baby gate. Have your puppy on a leash and Gentle Leader® so that you can control her behavior.

Entice your puppy to sit or down using the procedures in this book. Your goal is to teach your puppy that she can be calm and in control when your cat is nearby, rather than engaging in frenzied chasing.

If your puppy is just too frantic with your cat that close, then begin this process with your cat farther away. You might also let your puppy sniff some old towels that you have rubbed your cat with. This may help your puppy satisfy her curiosity about your cat.

Alternatively, if your puppy is accepting her crate, you can put her in it, and using tidbits or toys, encourage your cat to approach.

Find a variety of locations to stage these practice sessions. Move the baby gate to different doorways or try the sliding screen door to the backyard (puppy outside). An exercise pen or puppy playpen for holding your puppy provide other options to stage training sessions.

If you can't seem to make progress with this approach, or if you believe your puppy is intent on harming your cat, ask your veterinarian for a referral to a certified behaviorist or trainer.

 ## Keep Bad Habits from Developing

Minimize your puppy's chances to chase and harass your cat. Supervise their interactions, and do not leave your puppy and your cat alone together. If your puppy gets in the habit of behaving in unacceptable ways toward your cat, it will interfere with and prolong your puppy learning good behavior.

Meet Your Puppy's and Your Cat's
Behavioral and Developmental Needs

If your cat is quite upset about your puppy's presence, has started to hide, and is afraid to move around the house, this is a quality of life issue you need to address. You must be better about supervising your puppy, creating escape places for your cat and work more on a gradual introduction.

Baby gates usually are a good choice, because most cats can jump over them and most puppies cannot. Just as with your adult dogs, try to keep your cat's routines the same and find quality time for your cat.

You may need to make adjustments in where your cat's food, water and litterboxes are located. Putting your cat's food and water in a high place, such as a counter or shelf will prevent your puppy from stealing your cat's food or bothering her while she's eating.

Your puppy will likely find the contents of the litterbox quite appealing. It's very difficult to find a barrier that will allow your cat access to the box while keeping your puppy out, unless you have a large puppy and a small cat. Gating off the litterbox room with a baby gate may work, as long as your cat can easily negotiate the gate. Be sure your cat has unobstructed access to the box, or housesoiling may result. Close supervision of your puppy may be your best alternative. Never allow your puppy to surprise or harass your cat while she's in the litterbox.

As your puppy learns to respect your cat, the two may enjoy playing together. However, don't expect either your cat or your other dogs to completely meet your puppy's need for play and social time. That's your responsibility. Be sure that you are giving your puppy sufficient social time, play time, and engaging her in mentally stimulating activities–such as basic training.

 ## Use the "Take-Away" Method
to Discourage Behaviors You Don't Like

If your puppy is bothering your cat, first try to interest your puppy in another form of play. If she can't be distracted, put your puppy in a brief time out (as described under Preventing Chaos at the Door). It's rare that your cat will be the one harassing your puppy, but if he does, your cat goes in the time out.

 ## Make Discipline the Last Resort and Use It Correctly

Aversive approaches have the same disadvantages with cat-puppy problems as they do with dog-puppy problems. You don't want either pet to associate "bad things" with the presence of the other. You can try squirting your puppy with water for her cat-harassment if the "take-away" method doesn't work. If the water momentarily stops the behavior, you must immediately get your puppy engaged in doing something else.

If the water method doesn't work, talk to your veterinarian about a referral to a certified behaviorist or trainer. If it seems that you are constantly having to discipline your puppy for her behavior toward your cat, this is a warning sign. Talk to a behavior professional who can help you get back on track.

Chapter 8
Have Shoe, Will Chew: Managing Your Puppy's Need to Chew

 Understanding Chewing Behavior

Chewing is what puppies do. It's just as natural and normal as babies wetting their diapers. You may be prepared to deal with some chewing, but you may be surprised at how much your puppy chews, how many different things he can find to chew on, and how long the chewing stage lasts.

Puppies chew for several reasons, one of which is teething. Puppies chew and put things in their mouths to explore their world, and when playing. Do not expect chewing to stop at six months of age when your puppy has most of his adult teeth. The chewing stage can last until a dog is a year old or more, so don't be surprised if your year old dog still finds your shoes attractive.

Having realistic expectations won't stop your puppy from chewing but it may help you to get through this stage in a better frame of mind. Remember two truisms:

- expect to lose something of value, either sentimental or monetary, to your puppy's teeth
- on any given day, any puppy can turn anything into a chew toy

Let's see how dealing with chewing behavior can be put in the framework of the Five-Step Positive Proaction Plan.

 Help Your Puppy Do the Right Thing

Reward Your Puppy for Chewing on His Toys
Too often your attention may be focused on your puppy when he's doing the wrong thing rather than the right one. When he's quietly

chewing on a chewie you've given him, gently pet him and praise him quietly. You want to let him know how pleased you are with his behavior. The more consistent you are in rewarding this behavior, the stronger it will become.

 ## Keep Bad Habits from Developing

Puppy-proof the House
If you are a parent, you are in the habit of keeping the things you don't want your kids to have out of their reach. You must do the same thing for your puppy. Don't leave clothes, shoes and other items lying around that most any puppy would consider to be great things to chew on. Remember the truism from before—anything can be a chew toy from your puppy's point of view. For things that can't be placed out of reach, such as furniture, remote punishers or "booby-traps" are another option. Try making objects taste bad using one of the many products available at pet stores.

Supervise Your Puppy, and Manage His Environment so that He Doesn't have the Chance to Chew on Things He Shouldn't
You know that if you leave your puppy alone, unsupervised for any length of time, he will find something to chew on. This can be dangerous because your puppy can get into toxic or poisonous substances or chew on electrical cords. So, don't do it!! Use baby gates or close doors to rooms to keep your puppy in sight at all times when you are home.

If you will be crating your puppy when you are gone, refer to the section on crate training to learn how to acclimate your puppy to a crate. If you choose not to use a crate, your puppy can be confined in a puppy-proofed area.

 ## Meet Your Puppy's Behavioral and Developmental Needs

The goal of dealing with normal puppy chewing behavior is not to stop him from chewing, because we couldn't even if we tried, but rather to teach him what things you want him to chew. This requires meeting your puppy's needs with the type and number of chew toys you provide him.

Provide Good Chew Toys

Puppies need a variety of textures to chew. They will quickly become bored with just one type of chewie. Items that make good chew toys are often different from toys that puppies like to play with in other ways. Toys that can be carried around the house, pounced on, or shaken are good for playing fetch but may not be good for chewing.

Good chew toys are somewhat "squishy," or can be made so. We love the kinds of toys that can be filled with various goodies and treats. These toys are durable and have a squishy feel that appeals to most puppies. Visit our Web site at www.AnimalBehaviorAssociates.com to see a selection of Busy Buddy® toys from Premier® and more from the KONG™ company. Rawhides are another possibility, but ask your veterinarian for the type and quantity he or she recommends. Some are impregnated with substances that will help clean your dog's teeth.

Most puppies enjoy Booda Bones™, which are made from pressed cornstarch and are easily digestible. Some chewies, such as Nyla-Bones™ can be made more palatable by soaking them in beef broth, or rubbing them with meat or cheese.

Freezing a wet washcloth tied in a knot may provide soothing cold for inflamed gums during teething, as will frozen baby carrots and ice cubes. You may need to experiment with different types of chewies to see which ones your puppy prefers.

Toys that are Not Recommended

Avoid any kind of bones, such as chicken bones, that can splinter. These can become lodged anywhere in your puppy's throat or intestinal tract and do lots of damage. Avoid cow hooves, as they can cause your dog's teeth to crack, and pig's ears as they can carry salmonella.

Be careful with squeaky toys. Puppies who are particularly into chewing can destroy the toy and swallow the squeaker. Puppies can sometimes ingest large pieces of toys, including whole socks, or pieces of fleece from soft toys. If you leave your puppy alone with a chew toy, make sure it is safe.

Rotate the Toys You make Available

At Christmas time it's always fun to get the ornaments and decorations out from storage. You haven't seen them in a year, and it's almost like seeing them for the first time. When all of a puppy's toys are always available, they often lose their appeal because your puppy sees them everyday. By rotating your puppy's stockpile of toys, old ones can become more interesting and exciting. Have two or three chew toys available one day, pick those up and put two or three others out the next day.

Provide your Puppy with Plenty of Exercise and Play Time
Because puppies find chewing a form of exercise and play, giving your puppy other opportunities for these behaviors may decrease his chewing time. Take your puppy for walks, play fetch with him in the backyard and work on the training exercises you are learning in puppy class. Even tug games are fine, as long as your puppy never puts teeth on skin, and will drop or release his hold on the toy when asked. Follow the instructions later in this book on how to teach your puppy to "give."

 ## Use the "Take-Away" Method to Discourage Behaviors You Don't Like

Substitute Acceptable Chewies for "Off Limit" Items
This isn't exactly the same thing as the "take-away" method, but it still is a good way of reacting when you find your puppy chewing on something he shouldn't. Don't make a big deal out of the situation, but calmly take away what your puppy shouldn't have, and replace it with one of his own toys or chewies. It may be helpful if you move him away from the area where he was chewing, so you change his focus as well.

 ## Make Discipline the Last Resort and Use it Correctly

Don't Try to "Discipline" After the Fact
Never, ever take your puppy and show him what he's chewed on and try to punish him when you haven't actually seen him chewing. Puppies do not process information like children do. They cannot be shown the results of their destructive chewing and make the connection with the actual chewing *behavior* they did minutes or hours before.

In your puppy's eyes, you will be an unpredictable, untrustworthy individual who for unknown reasons drags him to different spots around the house and becomes angry and unpleasant to be around.

You may be tempted to assume your puppy "knows he's done wrong" but puppies do not have a moral sense of right and wrong. They don't know that it is "wrong" (in your eyes, not theirs!) to chew shoes, and "right" to chew bones. What you view as "guilty looks" are simply submissive behaviors resulting from your puppy being fearful of your angry behavior.

Any Discipline Should be Remote Rather than Interactive
"Discipline," or more accurately "punishment" that is delivered by you (interactive) has many drawbacks. First, your puppy will quickly learn that when you aren't around, nothing bad happens when he chews on your shoes, so he will continue to do so in your absence. For punishment to be effective, it must be delivered both *immediately* and *consistently.* It is virtually impossible to do either if you try to deliver the punishment. For this reason, it is far better to use remote punishers—booby traps or things that give your puppy a bad experience.

Examples of remote punishers include:

- Snappy Trainers™, which are modified, harmless versions of mousetraps
- Substances that give objects an uncomfortably hot or bitter taste, such as Bitter Apple™
- Motion detectors such as a Scraminal™ that emit startling noises and/or flashing lights
- A new motion detector called a SSSCAT®, emits a harmless spray, both the spray and the WHOOSHING noise startle the puppy

Many of these products are available at our Web site www.AnimalBehaviorAssociates.com, or see the Order Form in the back of the book.

Chapter 9
Puppy Mouthing and Nipping

 ## Why Puppies Chew on Hands

Just as they like to chew, puppies like to put your hands in their mouths. This is a normal and unavoidable puppy behavior. Puppies explore their world, and play using their mouths. Teething also motivates puppies to want to mouth your hands, as the soft pressure probably feels good on their gums.

Many behaviorists feel that puppies outgrow the tendency to want to chew on hands, even if you do nothing at all to *discourage* it, as long as you do not inadvertently *encourage* or reinforce the behavior. These behaviors are usually easily dealt with using our Five-Step Positive Proaction Plan.

 ## Help Your Puppy Do the Right Thing

If your puppy wants to put your hand in her mouth whenever you try to touch her, get in the habit of petting with one hand, while holding a small chewie or soft toy for your puppy with the other. This keeps her mouth busy and away from the temptation of your hand.

You may need to experiment until you find a chewie or toy she likes. As your puppy grows up and out of the mouthy stage, you'll be able to pet her without always having a chewie handy.

You might also find that if you pet your puppy on her shoulders or under her chin, rather than reaching over her head, she'll be less likely to want to put your hand in her mouth.

 ## Keep Bad Habits from Developing

Don't be tempted to let your puppy chew on your fingers just because it's normal puppy behavior or because you think it's cute. Don't tease your puppy with your fingers, or encourage her to use your hands or other body parts as chew toys.

Meet Your Puppy's Behavioral and Developmental Needs

You've already learned the tremendous need puppies have to chew. Your puppy may be more likely to want to use your hand as a chewie if she doesn't have enough opportunities to chew other things. Refer to the Have Shoe Will Chew chapter to make sure you are meeting your puppy's behavioral needs.

 ### Use the "Take-Away" Method to Discourage Behaviors You Don't Like

What does your puppy want when she nips and chews on your hands? Usually it's attention and the chance to play with you. These are the things that you want to take away as a consequence of her nipping.

When your puppy puts her teeth on your skin to the point of discomfort, either stop petting her, or get up and walk away from her. It may be more effective if you say "OUCH" or "OWWW" in a high-pitched voice as you remove your hand or walk away. This somewhat resembles a "YIP" another puppy might give in the same circumstances. If you find this noise just excites your puppy more, don't use it.

After a minute or two, return to your puppy and begin to calmly play with her or pet her. If she nips, repeat the procedure. She must have the opportunity to learn that nipping makes you go away, while having a soft mouth and not hurting you causes you to stay and play with her.

 ### Make Discipline the Last Resort and Use it Correctly

Discipline really isn't necessary and can do more harm than good. The other four parts of the Plan usually work quite well in discouraging and managing normal puppy nipping. If your puppy is the rare exception, you may need to talk to your veterinarian for a referral to a certified behaviorist or trainer for more specialized assistance.

Never, ever stuff your hand in your puppy's mouth in an attempt to teach her nipping is bad. Puppies have literally choked to death from this procedure.

Never, ever hit your puppy about the face with your hand. This includes "tapping" her on the nose with a few fingers. Your puppy may view this as more play rather than discipline. It's also too easy for the "tapping" to become too hard if you are angry or frustrated. Using your hands for discipline will either make your puppy afraid of your hands or encourage her to bite at them even more, or both.

Do not scruff shake or "alpha roll" your puppy. These are confrontational techniques that can result in fear and aggression problems. They can be extremely intimidating to many puppies, and are unnecessary for dealing with this normal, developmental behavior. Contrary to popular literature, these techniques **do not** mimic dog or wolf behavior, and they are much too harsh for dealing with puppies.

Chapter 10
Preventing Chaos at the Door

Puppies aren't born knowing what the doorbell means, but they learn extremely quickly. Within a few short weeks or a month, your puppy will get excited because he knows the doorbell means visitors.

You can prevent bad habits such as jumping up on people, dashing out the door, or barking excessively, by teaching your pup what you want him to do when the doorbell rings.

 ## Help Your Puppy Do the Right Thing

Keep a container of tidbits near the door, but out of your puppy's reach. When your puppy accompanies you to the door, have a treat ready, and lure him into a sit (See Chapter 12). Give your visitors treats and ask them to do the same thing.

Practice with family members acting as visitors. Have them ring the doorbell, come inside and immediately ask your puppy to sit. Repeat these practice sessions frequently so that your puppy gets in the habit of sitting at the door, no matter who comes to visit.

If your puppy is too excited to sit, start by just putting the treats on the floor. Your puppy can't be jumping on people if he's treasure hunting instead! Another option is to throw a toy for your pup until he calms down sufficiently to be able to sit.

You may need to put a leash on your puppy to prevent him from dashing out the door. Use a leash rather than grabbing at your puppy's neck or collar.

A Gentle Leader® helps you control your puppy even more and will make it easier for you to lure your puppy with the tidbits. Gentle Leaders® are available at our Web site, www.AnimalBehaviorAssociates.com, and you can learn more about them at www.Premier.com.

Keep Bad Habits from Developing

Never encourage your puppy to get excited when he sees or hears something outside. Asking your puppy, "What's that? What do you hear? Let's go see!!," will only increase his arousal when you want to be working on decreasing it.

Prevent your children from running and screaming when the doorbell rings, inciting your puppy to bark and chase them. Rather than yelling at your puppy to "STOP, BE QUIET," instead calmly ask him to come to you. Or, don't say anything until you can get to the door and implement procedures to control your puppy.

 ## Meet Your Puppy's Behavioral
and Developmental Needs

Socialization will help prevent your puppy from being fearful or threatening toward people he doesn't know. The more people your puppy meets, the better. Your puppy needs to be introduced to a wide circle of different folks. Refer back to the section on socialization for details.

 ## Use the "Take-Away" Method to
Discourage Behaviors You Don't Like

If your puppy jumps on visitors, instruct them to turn and walk away from him. Your puppy is jumping because he wants attention. By walking away, your visitors are taking away his chance to get what he wants.

You can consider putting your puppy in a brief time-out if he's really uncontrollable or nips at visitors. The time-out location needs to be close by, so that your puppy can associate his misbehavior with the time-out consequence.

A puppy-proofed coat closet or powder room near your door might be a great spot. Quickly but gently pick your puppy up, or snap his leash on and lead him to the area. Leave him there for no more than three minutes and let him out.

Use treats and/or your leash and Gentle Leader® to again encourage him to sit. Chances are he'll be a bit subdued by his closet experience and more likely to respond to your directions.

 ## Make Discipline the Last Resort and Use it Correctly

It is much better to use the "take-away" method rather than intimidation or painful procedures to stop your puppy from jumping up. Do not hold or squeeze his front paws, knee him in the chest, or step on his back feet.

With these procedures, you run the risk of your puppy learning not to enjoy meeting new people. This is a far more serious problem than jumping up.

For more detailed information about preventing chaos at the door, listen to our audio CD, "Managing Chaos at the Door," available at our web site www.AnimalBehaviorAssociates.com, or see the Order Form at the back of this book.

You can also teach your puppy to automatically lie down at the designated spot when the doorbell rings, using an innovative product called Treat and Train®. The Treat and Train® is available from Sharper Image Corporation, or contact Animal Behavior Associates for more information.

Chapter 11
Teach Your Puppy to Enjoy Handling, Mild Restraint and Grooming

 ## Accustoming Your Puppy to Being Held and Handled

Being held, restrained and having her body examined and groomed should be enjoyable experiences for your puppy. Some puppies may be fearful at first, while others may decide they don't want to take the time to hold still long enough, and will struggle to be left alone.

Getting in a wrestling match with your puppy will not be helpful. Instead, create an expectation that being held and having body parts touched are enjoyable experiences.

Begin by gently cradling your puppy in your arms or between your legs (depending on her size and reaction) while offering her a tidbit. Release your puppy before she begins to struggle. This should only be for a few seconds at first.

When the puppy learns that cradling means a tidbit, she should react positively when you reach to pick her up, perhaps even sniffing around looking for her tidbit. This is your signal that you can increase the time you hold and cradle the puppy, while still intermittently giving her treats.

For some puppies, the process can progress rapidly. You should be able to use fewer treats as your puppy becomes accustomed to this procedure. If your puppy becomes impatient and struggles to get loose, hold her until she is still for just a second or two. Teach her being still earns freedom, struggling does not.

Be cautious with this approach however. If your puppy is fearful, holding her tighter may increase her fear. In this case, you will need more repetitions with briefer time periods to increase your puppy's confidence.

As you cradle your puppy, gently massage her. Lightly squeeze her legs and paws, rub her neck and torso, stroke her ears and head. Most puppies will think this feels pretty special, and will relax. If your puppy wants to nibble your hand, give her a soft toy or chewie to hold in her mouth instead.

If your puppy is too excited to be able to relax, don't worry about it. Instead, for a while practice your handling only when your puppy is tired or sleepy. When your puppy becomes easier to handle, try situations that are a bit more difficult such as when your puppy would rather be doing something else.

Begin to add more experiences. Open your puppy's mouth and put a treat in it. Lift up her ear, look inside, and give her a tidbit. Gently touch your puppy's "privates" while praising her and giving her a goodie. The goal is for your puppy to be relaxed about having any part of her body touched.

 ## Introducing Your Puppy to Grooming Procedures

The next step is to introduce your puppy to a brush, comb, toothbrush, and other tools you will use for grooming and dental care. Let your puppy look at and sniff these objects to satisfy her curiosity and reduce any fear.

At first, gently run the brush over her back, or put the toothbrush against her teeth. You want your puppy to adjust to the feel of these items against her body. Don't be in a hurry to actually accomplish any brushing. Be generous with treats and gentle petting so your puppy learns there is nothing to fear.

If your puppy wants to chew on the brush or comb, give her a small chew toy to keep her mouth busy. Make the brushing gentle at first, and don't worry too much about combing out tangles until your puppy is used to the process. You don't want her first few experiences with grooming to be unpleasant.

Practice with your puppy regularly—at least several times a week. If your puppy only sees the brush, comb, or toothbrush every now and then, she won't become familiar and at ease with these tools and procedures.

The time you spend practicing body handling and body care procedures will pay off big time as your puppy matures. Think how easy it will be if you have to pull a thorn out of your puppy's foot, or clean her ears if she has learned to relax and be still. It isn't fun for you or your puppy if handling always becomes a wrestling match. If you work consistently with these exercises, you can avoid this unpleasantness.

Your veterinarian or trainer may suggest other handling exercises. If you practice these gentle handling exercises, there is absolutely no reason to have a puppy who won't allow you to touch her feet, brush her or look in her mouth.

 ## Making Nail Trims a "Good Thing"

If you've ever had a dog who did not like to have her nails cut, you know what a problem this can be. Puppies need to learn early on that having their feet touched and held is not a bad thing. If a puppy's first experience with a nail trim is a bad one, it can result in her hating nail trims for the rest of her life.

Begin by picking up your puppy's foot and immediately offering a tidbit with the other hand. Repeat until your puppy is not anxious or struggling and gives signs that she is either expecting a tidbit or is relaxing her leg because she knows you are going to pick it up. If you wish, use a phrase such as, "Let me see your paw" to cue this behavior.

Once your puppy is relaxed with her paw in your hand, require your puppy to leave it there for a second or two before giving her the treat. If she removes her paw, withhold the treat, pick up the paw again and repeat. Gradually increase the amount of time she must hold her paw on your hand before she can receive the treat.

Next, pick up your puppy's paw and gently squeeze it while offering a tidbit. At first, give your puppy the tidbit even if she tries to withdraw her paw from the pressure. Chances are, the tidbit will help her relax and she will stop trying to withdraw her paw. To get your puppy used to continued squeezing, squeeze for a few seconds, then reward her with a tidbit.

The next step is to get your puppy used to the feel of the metal clippers against her nails. Gently tap each nail on a foot with the clippers. Each tap should be followed by a tidbit. You may only be able to work with one foot, or perhaps even one nail per practice session. Keep these work sessions short so your puppy doesn't get tired or frustrated. Tap each nail on all four feet before attempting to clip any nails.

After tapping a nail, quickly trim the sharp tip, release the foot, and give your pup a tidbit. Clip only the sharp, bloodless tip of the nail. Repeat with each nail. After more practice, you should be able to clip all the nails on one foot before rewarding your puppy, but at first, small steps and lots of reinforcement are important. If you haven't cut nails before, **ask your veterinarian** to show you how so you don't hurt your puppy. If your puppy has black nails, it's especially important that someone show you the proper technique.

 ## The Value of these Procedures

This entire process may take 10 or 12 sessions, before you complete a full nail trim, but it is well worth it to end up with a puppy who is calm and relaxed when you cut her nails. You'll be able to use fewer treats as your puppy gets used to the procedures, but never phase out the treats completely. Remember to make the treats part of the nail trimming process, and not just rewards for good behavior at the end.

Trimming your puppy's nails is not a life or death procedure–it doesn't have to be accomplished on a rigid time schedule. If you, your puppy's veterinarian or groomer is trying to trim nails, and your puppy becomes very agitated, upset and struggles to get away, don't insist on completing the procedure. Increasing your restraint and forcing the puppy to accept something that is clearly terrifying her is counterproductive and will result in your puppy hating nail trims. Just STOP–and instead of forcing the issue, take the time to gradually acclimate your puppy to nail trims using the step-by-step procedures described.

Chapter 12
Teaching Your Puppy Basic Manners

This chapter introduces you to training techniques you should use to teach your puppy behaviors you'll want him to do every day. You should start training your puppy immediately, as soon as he comes home. Formal training sessions aren't always necessary—just incorporate training into your daily interactions and play time.

In addition to training at home, enroll your puppy in a puppy class. Puppy classes provide unbeatable opportunities for socialization, and the instructor will be able to provide individualized assistance and help you advance beyond the beginning training methods provided here.

Select a class and instructor using the guidelines in Chapter 14.

 ## Teaching Your Puppy "Gentle"

Being able to take treats gently from your hand is an important skill for your puppy to learn. When you give your puppy treats in training, for socialization, and just as a special gift, you'll want him to leave your fingers intact! If you have children, it is especially important for your puppy to learn early on how to take treats without hurting fingers.

Start by holding a tidbit in your fist, with just a small piece of it showing between your fingers. Your puppy will want the tidbit, and will try a variety of ways to obtain it. He may paw at your hand, nip you, try to grab the treat, or wrap his paws around your hand.

The only acceptable behaviors that result in you giving your puppy the treat are not touching your hand at all, or licking it. If your puppy tries any of the other behaviors mentioned, put the hand with the treat in it behind your back for a few seconds, then try again.

If you have a creative puppy who barks at you, put your hand behind your back and turn your head to the side so you aren't looking at him. This tells your puppy you have "tuned him out" and have removed him chance to get the treat. For an extremely persistent puppy, you may need to walk away from him and try again a few minutes later.

Your puppy will be confused and a little frustrated because he doesn't know what to do to get the treat. Put your hand out again. If your puppy hesitates a second and doesn't try to get the treat, *immediately* open your hand and offer it to him.

If he immediately jumps on your hand or bites at it, put your hand behind your back as many times as you need to until you get that moment of hesitation or a lick. If after four or five attempts, he still isn't getting it, then get up and walk away from him. Try again in a minute or two.

The trick is not to become frustrated and resort to discipline, and not to expect too much at first. Let your puppy have the tidbit if he hesitates just an instant. Once he is rewarded for a tiny bit of success, he'll more quickly get the idea of what you want.

When he's starting to get the hang of it and not biting at your hand, say "gentle" as you offer the treat. The idea is for the word "gentle" to cue the behavior you want. At this point require that your puppy hold back for a bit longer after you say "gentle" before you give him the tidbit. Don't prolong the time to getting the treat excessively or you'll confuse your puppy and he won't understand what "gentle" means.

After your puppy is doing well with adults, make sure that you help your children practice this exercise. Smaller children will need adult assistance. Hold the child's hand atop or inside of your own as your offer the treat. Don't assume that just because your puppy has learned the behavior with you, he will automatically do the same with your kids or other adults. You must help him generalize the same behavior to everyone who has a treat for him. A puppy class is extremely valuable to help your puppy generalize because you have easy access to people who will respond to your puppy the same way you do.

Use the Lure-Reward Method to Teach Sit

Rather than pushing and pulling your puppy into a sit or down position, we prefer a method that prompts your puppy to do the behavior on his own. This procedure is called "lure-reward," because you'll use something the puppy wants, most often a tidbit, to lure your puppy into a particular position and then reward him when he gets there.

For example, to get your puppy to sit, hold a tidbit directly above your puppy's nose, and slowly move it backward. As your puppy tips his head back to follow the treat, in order to keep his balance, it is likely his rear will fold into a sit. When this happens *immediately* give him the treat to reward the behavior. Thus, lure-reward.

After a few attempts, your puppy should be sitting fairly reliably when you hold the lure over his head. At this point, you can say the word "sit" as you present the lure but *before* your puppy starts to sit.

Don't be tempted to start saying "sit" before your puppy has gotten the idea of what to do when he sees the treat. If you are saying "sit" while your puppy is pawing at your hand for example, this will only confuse your puppy.

The next step is to fade, or gradually make the lure less visible, so your puppy is responding to "sit" rather than the appearance of the treat. Fading the treat is done in a series of steps, such as:

❑ Rather than showing your pup the lure, hold it in your fist–pup learns he can still get the tidbit even if he doesn't see it

❑ Hold the treat in your other hand, or pull it from your pocket, or even have someone else give him the treat (as long as he still receives it *immediately*)-pup learns not only does the treat not need to be visible, it can even come from somewhere else.

Your hand movement must also be faded. Say "sit" and hesitate a second or two to see if your pup will respond without also needing to see the movement of your hand. Don't wait too long at first. If your pup doesn't sit, make a small movement with your hand, and reward the sitting response. Hand movement can be faded as follows:

❑ Rather than bringing your fist all the way to your puppy's nose, only move it half way.

❑ Continue decreasing how much you move your hand toward your pup until you are making only a slight forward movement.

❑ Fade out all hand motion.

If your puppy fails to sit as you are fading the lure, you might have tried to fade the lure too quickly. If that happens, back up a step, and add another intermediate step in the fading process. After you say "sit," be sure to hesitate a second to see if he's going to do it without the lure. If you don't completely fade the lure, your pup will only sit when he sees the food, or when he sees your hand move.

To get your puppy to hold a sitting position, refer to the section on teaching your puppy to hold a position.

Use the Lure-Reward Method to Teach Down

The down follows naturally from the sit. Lure your puppy into a sitting position first. Next, slowly move the treat to the floor, and curve it around behind one front leg. You may need to experiment to see if your puppy more easily follows the treat if you move it to his right or his left. As he turns his upper body to follow the treat, gently help him shift onto the opposite hip with your other hand. He'll end up in a more relaxed position if he's lying on one hip rather than on his breast-bone. As soon as he's lying down, let him take the treat from your hand.

Don't get frustrated with your puppy in the initial stages. Let your puppy figure out what will get him the treat. He may begin to paw at your hand or bark at you. It may take four or five tries or a minute or two until you can get him into the down position.

Some puppies do better if you move the treat straight down, to a position between their front legs, and then slowly drag it forward. Your puppy will be more likely to end up in the "breastbone position" with this method. Try getting your puppy to shift onto one hip by moving the treat behind one front leg, and/or gently push him over on his hip.

If you both are really "stuck" then reward your puppy for following the treat even part way. With each succeeding step, require him to follow it just a little further, so that you are rewarding incremental progress, or "baby steps," rather than requiring him to get all the way down before being rewarded. This approach will prevent your puppy from giving up because he isn't getting his reward.

Initially, do not say "down" as you lure your puppy. However, when your puppy is reliably lying down in response to the lure, say the word "down" as you present the lure but **before** your puppy starts to lie down.

Pick your cue word carefully for the down. You cannot have "down" mean both lie down and "get off" or "don't jump." Most people find it easiest to say "down" for lying down, and "off" for getting off of the furniture or people.

As with the sit, you must also fade the treat, and fade your hand motion in a series of steps. Refer to the previous page on sitting to learn how to do this.

 ## Getting Your Puppy to Hold the Position

To encourage your puppy to hold both "sit" and "down" longer than momentarily, begin to add a delay before giving your puppy his tidbit after you get him in the position you want. Don't use the "stay" command yet, but just use a hand gesture–palm open and facing your puppy. This puts a small natural barrier between you and him and encourages him to stay put.

Puppies have such short attention spans, it's not realistic to expect them to stay for minutes at a time, as adult dogs can do. For now, work on getting your puppy to sit or down in all kinds of locations, despite distractions for 30 seconds or so.

Teaching "stay" requires extreme consistency, and a release word that tells your puppy when he can get up. Stay will have no meaning to your puppy if you don't make it clear to your puppy when the "stay" is over. Stay is usually formally taught in a beginning training class.

Teach Your Puppy to Come When Called

For your puppy to learn to come reliably no matter where he is or what he is doing, he must think that coming when called is about the most fun he could possibly have in his whole life. You must never, ever call your puppy and then do something unpleasant such as discipline him, give him a bath, or give him a pill.

If you don't think your puppy is going to come when you call him because he is too far away or too distracted, then don't use the "come" word. Either go and get him or entice him to come to you by running away from him, shaking the treat bag or offering him a toy.

It may be easier to start teaching the come if you have a helper. Have your helper gently restrain your puppy by holding him with hands on his chest. Stand or crouch down in front of your puppy, show your puppy a treat, talk to him excitedly, and walk 5 or 6 feet away from him. Crouch or sit down on the floor and call your puppy in the most excited tone of voice you can manage. Say your puppy's name followed by the word "come" or "here," whichever word you prefer. Clap your hands, and pat the floor to get your puppy excited.

While your puppy is moving toward you, make sure the treat or toy is visible, and move the lure all the way into your body. Don't reward your puppy at arm's length, but make sure he comes all the way to you. Do not grab or reach for your puppy–let him come to you all by himself. When he gets to you, touch his collar or neck and give him the tidbit.

When you are first teaching this behavior, make sure your puppy gets a reward every single time you call him. The reward should be more than just praise and petting. When you are sure he has the idea, give him a tidbit maybe 50–75% of the time, but always praise and pet him.

Don't be tempted to test how well he is doing by calling him from long distances at first. Set up lots of practice sessions in the house and the yard and call your puppy from only a few feet away at first.

Your family can practice "round robin" recalls by sitting in a circle. Have as much distance between family members as you think your puppy can successfully negotiate when he is called. Each person in turn calls the puppy and rewards him. Puppy classes are another great opportunity to practice coming when called, despite distractions.

If you will be practicing in open areas, make sure your puppy is on a long line or leash so he can't escape if he decides not to come to someone.

If you are having trouble with your puppy coming when called, make it easier for him to do so. Practice over and over again in quiet surroundings and from short distances away from your puppy. Make sure the reward for coming is something your puppy likes intensely. Most problems with coming when called result from expecting too much from your puppy too soon. It's very important that you practice many times in easy situations, and take "baby steps" to more distracting settings.

 ## Teach Your Puppy to "Give"

Few puppies try to threateningly defend their possessions, so now is a great time to teach your puppy to give up his toys or chewies when asked. You can start by getting your puppy used to you holding onto things while he chews on them. While your puppy chews a rawhide, or a plastic bone, different family members should hold on to the opposite end.

To prevent possessiveness problems, you want to create the expectation for your puppy that whenever you do take his chewie or toy away, something good is in it for him. When your puppy is chewing on something, approach him in a nonthreatening manner, tell him "Give", and *immediately* show him a tidbit. He will most likely stop chewing on his toy to take the treat. Take his toy, and give him the tidbit. This exercise teaches your puppy that when you say "Give" if he drops what he has, you'll give him something even better.

After a few practice sessions, you might see that your puppy begins to automatically drop the toy when you say "Give." Now it's time to fade the treat as the cue. Say "Give," wait a few seconds without showing him the treat. You want your puppy to drop his toy in response to "Give," without the behavior being cued by the tidbit.

If he doesn't, move your hand as though you are going to show him a treat, and wait to see if he drops the toy. If not, perhaps you need to practice a little more by prompting the behavior with the tidbit. As we did with teaching "sit" and "down," you need to convince your puppy that a treat is always possible, even if he doesn't see it right away.

Another technique is to take your puppy's toy away, and give it back to him with something special added. If he's chewing on a rawhide or plastic bone, take it away, rub it with a small bit of cheese spread or margarine and give it back to him.

Add more goodies to a Goodie Ship® or Busy Buddy® toy, or pull some of the treats partially out so your puppy can more easily get to them. This creates an expectation for your puppy that giving his toys to you is a good thing.

"Give" can also mean "give up your food bowl." Teach your puppy not to guard his food by walking by and dropping a tidbit in his dish when he is eating. When he seems to be happy about your approach, say "Give," offer your pup a treat, pick up the dish, put something special in it, and return it to your puppy. You can also hand-feed your puppy from his dish from time to time.

All family members should practice teaching "Give." Young children may need help from an adult. Use the same sort of techniques described in the "Teaching Gentle" section.

Teach Your Puppy to Walk Nicely

Puppies do not yet need to learn how to heel. Heeling means that your puppy stays right next to your leg, not a step ahead, not a step behind, and never interferes with your movement.

You may never require your dog to be this precise when he walks with you. Perhaps all you want is for your dog not to pull on the leash, dash in front of you or circle around behind you. That's what we mean by walk nice.

Teach your puppy this behavior by first teaching him to pay attention to you when he is on leash. Stand next to your puppy with the leash in one hand, treats in the other. Fold the leash on itself so that you only have about 3 or 4 feet to work with. Hold your leash-hand against your body and leave it there. Don't allow your puppy to pull it forward, and don't jerk back on the leash. Watch your puppy closely. Whenever he looks up at you, and/or is standing near you so that the leash is loose, say "YES" and give him a treat. If he tries to pull forward or gets distracted, take a few steps backward without pulling/jerking on the leash. When your puppy looks up and the leash is loose, treat him.

When your puppy is standing on a loose leash by your side, looking at you, begin to walk forward. Say your puppy's name followed by "Walk nice," or "By me," or any other word you choose (probably not "heel"). As long as your puppy stays by your side and doesn't pull, he gets rewarded at short intervals with a YES, treats and praise. When you see your puppy moving forward and you know he is going to start pulling, STOP, AND STAND STILL. Wait until your puppy comes back to you, say YES, give him a treat and then move forward again.

This will be a dance–a step or two forward, stop, forward, stop, back up, etc. The goal is not to spend time walking, the goal is to teach your puppy to stay with you. While you are working on loose leash walking, you should not allow your puppy to pull when he is on leash.

Thus, leash walks for a while may not be a good source of exercise, as they will need to be training times. In the meantime, try to get your puppy his exercise in other ways–playing in the back yard or taking him to a fenced dog park if he is old enough. Play with him and tire him out before you try walking him on a leash.

Walk your puppy on either a flat collar or a Gentle Leader®. Choke chains or pinch collars are inappropriate for puppies.

A Gentle Leader® will prevent your puppy from charging forward while you train him to walk nicely. Because the Gentle Leader® fits on your puppy's head, not just his neck, it gives you much more control over your puppy's movements than you could possibly have with just a collar.

Because puppies tend to be more flexible and adaptable than adult dogs, it's a good idea to introduce the Gentle Leader® now rather than waiting until your puppy is older. You can purchase a Gentle Leader® from our Web site at www.AnimalBehaviorAssociates.com and learn more about the collar from www.Premier.com. And the Gentle Leader® doesn't cause pain as choke or pinch collars do.

Chapter 13
SUMMARY

This book has given you a good start on raising a behaviorally healthy puppy. These recommended procedures are a beginning not an end. While what you do during puppyhood is crucially important to your puppy's behavioral health, your responsibilities don't stop there.

Keeping your dog behaviorally healthy is a lifetime responsibility. This doesn't have to be a burden, but instead can be part of the joy of sharing life with a dog. A well-behaved dog can be so much more of an integral part of your life. She can accompany you on outings, vacations, and family activities such as soccer games. The better behaved she is, the more experiences she can share with you. The more experiences she shares, the better behaved and socialized she becomes. This creates an increasingly positive spiral resulting in a dog who is the companion you've dreamed of.

When problems arise, as they inevitably will, don't give up. Any relationship worth having is worth working on. Seek professional help sooner rather than later, and don't rely on advice from friends and relatives.

Your puppy deserves your best efforts to help her develop to her full potential. This puppy book gives you a good start in achieving that goal. Talk to your veterinarian, trainer, behaviorist or local animal shelter about fun activities you can participate in with your dog including agility, flyball, and freestyle. Or visit the American Kennel Club's Web site at www.akc.org for more information about companion dog sports.

We know not only from research, but also from experience, that dogs enrich our lives in ways even our closest human friends and family cannot. As Konrad Lorenz, the well known pioneer in behavioral research said, "The fidelity of a dog is a precious gift demanding no less binding moral responsibilities than the friendship of a human being. The bond with a true dog is as lasting as the ties of this earth can ever be."

Chapter 14
Guidelines for Choosing a Dog Trainer or Behavior Consultant

As we've mentioned, you may sometimes need professional help with your puppy's behavior. How do you know who to call? Do you need a dog trainer or a behaviorist? What's the difference? How do you choose one or the other from the pages and pages of listings in the telephone book?

What do dog trainers do?

A dog trainer works with you to teach your dog specific skills such as sitting when told, coming when called, and walking on a leash without pulling. Trainers often give advice or educate you about other training issues such as jumping up, crate training, or adjusting your dog's manners around others.

Trainers generally instruct you how to train your dog and supervise your training. Trainers at board-and-train facilities will train your dog themselves, without you being present (we don't generally recommend this approach). Some trainers work with other animals such as cats or horses, and do behavior consulting as well.

Expect to pay a fee for both training classes and individual, private training. Prices vary widely depending on where you live and the expertise and quality of the trainer.

What do behavior consultants do?

A behavior consultant is a person who works with you to manage, resolve or prevent specific behavior problems you may be having with your pet. These may include things such as aggression, fears and phobias, separation anxiety, or housesoiling. These are not "obedience" problems, and training classes or private training instruction won't help them.

Behavior consultants identify the cause of the problem and then recommend a plan to for you to implement to change the behavior. Consultants both tell you and show you what to do, but generally do not take your dog and work with her for you.

Behavior consultants may work with dogs, cats, or other species such as horses or birds. Some behavior consultants also do dog training.

Behavioral consultants use a variety of professional titles, including applied animal behaviorist, animal behaviorist, behavior specialist, dog psychologist, behaviorist, or veterinary behaviorist. Only board certified veterinarians may use the title veterinary behaviorist or veterinary behavior specialist. Only those certified by the Animal Behavior Society can use the term Certified Applied Animal Behaviorist. Anyone, regardless of training or experience, can use the other titles.

Behavior consultants also charge a fee for their services. Don't expect free advice, tips, or solutions in "25 words or less."

Where to Find Trainers and Behavior Consultants

You'll find both dog trainers and behaviorists listed in the telephone book or local pet publications. Rather than taking your chances in the phone directory, you are better off asking for a referral from your veterinarian or local animal shelter.

You can also find lists of certified pet dog trainers, certified applied animal behaviorists, and board certified veterinary behaviorists from the Web sites listed in the Resource section at the back of this book.

What does Certification Mean?

Quite a few new "certification" groups have appeared in the last few years, many of which are merely "certifying" graduates of their own training programs or schools. This type of certification has no validity or credibility and is not representative of a true professional certification. If someone says they are "certified," you should ask:

a. What group or organization does the certification come from? Credible certification programs are administered by independent professional organizations without ties to any specific training program or private school.

b. What are the criteria for certification? Credible certification programs should not require individuals to be graduates of any specific training program or school. Look for educational, experiential and ethical criteria, as well as required letters of recommendation, testing, and/ or professional review of the individual's work.

c. Is the certifying group associated with a training school or program? Credible certification programs are not associated with the program that trains the certificants.

d. Is any academic or college education required for certification? Individuals who have studied animal behavior at the college or graduate level are likely to be more knowledgeable.

Certification for Behavior Consultants

Academically trained behavior consultants can be certified by the Animal Behavior Society (ABS) or the American College of Veterinary Behaviorists (ACVB). The requirements for certification and a list of certified consultants can be found on the organizations' Web sites, which are listed in the Resource section of this book.

Certification for Dog Trainers

The Certification Council for Pet Dog Trainers (CCPDT) certifies dog trainers. The CCPDT works with an independent testing agency to administer a qualifying examination. The requirements for certification and a list of certified trainers can be found at the CCPDT's Web site. See the Resource section of this book.

Tips for Evaluating Dog Trainers and Behavior Consultants*

- Ask trainers from where and what type of training they received to become a professional trainer, how long they've been training professionally, and what kind of experience they have. Ask behavior consultants how they acquired their knowledge about behavior, and how they learned to be a behavior consultant. Look for academic training in animal learning and ethology, as well as supervised practical experience.
- Look for both trainers and behavior consultants who hold memberships in professional organizations and who pursue continuing edu-

cation. This indicates individuals who are interested in keeping current on the latest advances in their field.

- Both dog trainers and behavior consultants are really educating and training you, so look for good communication and social skills, and someone you feel comfortable talking to. Look for professionals who treat both people and dogs with respect and compassion. ABS, AVMA and the APDT all have ethical statements and guidelines on their Web sites.

- Choose trainers and behavior consultants who focus on encouraging and rewarding the right behavior with positive reinforcement, rather than relying on punishing or correcting undesirable ones. Both professionals should be willing to use whatever type of positive reinforcement works best for your dog, whether it is food, toys, petting or all three.

- Look for trainers who recognize the importance of you working with your own dog under their direction, rather than sending your dog somewhere for a professional trainer to train. Problem behavior often won't be manifested during a behavior consulting appointment (e.g., housesoiling), so it's up to you to work with your dog by following through with the recommendations given by the behavior consultant.

- Avoid anyone who guarantees results. Dogs are living creatures and no one knows enough about their behavior to guarantee outcomes. Some trainers and behavior consultants may guarantee satisfaction with their professional services, which is a different thing.

- Observe a training class without your dog. Are the dogs and people enjoying themselves? Talk to participants to see if they are comfortable with the training methods used. If a trainer won't let you sit in on a class, don't enroll. If, for confidentiality reasons, you are unable to observe a behavior consultation involving another pet owner, ask the behavior consultant for references, such as from veterinarians or shelters that use their services, or from former clients who have given permission to share information.

- Basic dog training can be accomplished without the use of choke chains, so don't enroll in a class that requires one. Head collars, buckle collars, and even certain types of harnesses are better choices.

- If either a trainer or behavior consultant tells you to do something to or with your dog that you don't feel comfortable with—don't do it! Don't be intimidated, bullied or shamed into doing something that you believe is not in the best interest of your dog. Don't allow anyone to work directly with your dog unless they first tell you what they are going to do. Don't be afraid to tell any trainer or behavior consultant to stop if they are doing something to your dog that you don't like.

- Because behavior problems can have medical causes, look for behavior consultants who encourage you to first consult with your veterinarian. Even if your pet doesn't look or act sick, medical conditions can affect your dog's behavior. Be wary of trainers or behavior consultants who insist on diet or other nutritional changes without relying on input from your veterinarian. Only veterinarians can prescribe medication for your dog.

- The Delta Society publishes a booklet entitled, <u>Professional Standards for Dog Trainers: Effective, Humane Principles</u>, which provides guidance in identifying humane and effective dog training principles. It is available from their Web site listed in the Resource section at the end of this book. Look for trainers who follow these principles.

- No matter how good the trainer or behavior consultant is, if you don't follow through with practice either in your everyday life with your dog, or with special practice sessions, you won't get the results you desire.

* Modified from an article by S. Hetts in <u>The Advocate</u>, 1996, <u>The American Humane Association</u>, and from S. Hetts, <u>Pet Behavior Protocols: What To Say, What To Do, When To Refer</u>, 1999, AAHA Press.

Chapter 15
Recommended Readings in Dog and Puppy Behavior

Donaldson, J. 1996. **The Culture Clash.** James & Kenneth Publ., Berkeley, CA.

Hart, B.L. and Hart, L.A. 1988. **The Perfect Puppy. How to Choose a Dog by Its Behavior**. W.H. Freeman, New York.

McConnell, Patricia, 2002. **The Other End of the Leash: Why We Do What We Do Around Dogs**. Ballantine Books, NY

Reid, P.J., 1996. **Excelerated Learning: Explaining in Plain English How Dogs Learn and How Best To Teach Them**. James and Kenneth Publishers, Oakland, CA.

Rutherford, C. and Neil, D.H. 1999. **How to Raise a Puppy You Can Live With, 3rd Ed.** Alpine Pub., Loveland.

Ryan, T. 1998. **The Toolbox for Remodeling Your Problem Dog.** Howell Book House, New York.

Silvani, Pia and Eckhardt, Lynn. 2005 (available in summer). **Raising Puppies and Children Together: A Parent's Guide.** TFH Publications, Neptune, NJ.

Tillman, P. 2000. **Clicking With Your Dog.** Sunshine Books, Waltham, MA.

Wright, J. C. and Lashnits, J.W. 1999. **The Dog Who Would Be King**. Rodale Press, Emmaus, PA.

Wright, J.C. and Lashnits, J.W. 2001. **Ain't Misbehavin'**. Rodale Press, Emmaus, PA.

Many of these books are available through our Web site, **www.AnimalBehaviorAssociates.com** or from **Dogwise**, a book and supply catalog, P. O. Box 2778, Wenatchee, WA 98807-2778, Phone 1-800-776-2665, or on the web at www.dogwise.com

RESOURCES

Web sites mentioned in this book

The Association of Pet Dog Trainers – www.apdt.com

The Certification Council for Pet Dog Trainers – www.ccpdt.org

The Delta Society – www.deltasociety.org (Go to the online store)

The Animal Behavior Society – www.animalbehavior.org

Diplomates of The American College of Veterinary Behaviorists – www.dacvb.org

Resources Available from Animal Behavior Associates, Inc.

Sign up TODAY at our Web site for "**Pet Behavior One Piece at a Time**"

Full of indispensable information on pet behavior, our **FREE** newsletter will help you be the pet parent your pet deserves.

All of the KONG® and Busy Buddy® toys mentioned in the book are available on our Web site, as are the other products mentioned in the book and described below.

If you need to schedule a behavior consultation with us, we offer in-home, office, telephone or email consultations. Details are available on our Web site, www.AnimalBehaviorAssociates.com.

We also have many free, downloadable articles about pet behavior and behavior problems, and Behavior Wellness reports on many topics from fears and phobias to aggression, in both dogs and cats.

"Just Behave: How to Get Your Dog to Do What You Want"

This two-hour live telecourse, complete with 13 pages of class notes, is a must for every dog owner. Both your dog's behavior and your relationship with your pet will improve when you take this course. You'll learn:

• What a behaviorally healthy dog is and how to have one
• Why thinking your dog is rebellious, spiteful or jealous can hurt your dog and your relationship

- A five-step plan to prevent and manage ANY behavioral issue you have with your dog
- How to prevent problems by meeting your dog's behavioral needs
- Much, much more!

Check our Web site, call or email for upcoming dates and current registration fees.

www.AnimalBehaviorAssociates.com
303-932-9095 phone; 303-932-2298 fax

"Canine Body Postures" $49.95

A 45-minute videotape that describes the communicative behavior of dogs; how to read dog behavior signals, recognize fearful and aggressive behavior, and influence the behavior of dogs. Also available in DVD format.

"What Dogs Need and How They Think" $5.00 each
"76 Ways to Get Your Dog to Do What You Want"

These 16-page booklets are packed with useful tips on how to make your relationship with your dog the best it can be.

You'll learn:
- Why it's a good idea to drop a tidbit when you walk by your resting dog
- Why you should ignore annoying behaviors from your dog
- You don't need to bully your dog to get him to do what you want
- Why every dog needs a private place away from the family

"Managing Chaos at the Door" $11.95

Listen to Drs. Hetts and Estep give you over ten different strategies to use when the doorbell rings and your dog goes berserk. Available either as an audio CD or presentation on CD illustrated with PowerPoint slides. Just like watching and listening to a live lecture! Viewable on any PC (sorry, not Mac compatible). You do not need PowerPoint to watch and listen to this presentation.

Additional copies of "Raising A Behaviorally Healthy Puppy"

Contact us for quantity pricing for use in puppy classes, animal shelters, veterinary practices or other pet businesses.

Gentle Leader® Headcollar $25.50

Power Steering for your dog! The #1 Recommended Headcollar for Dogs. Allows you to gain immediate, humane and effective control over your dog. Comfortable, painless and never chokes. We've used it for years and wouldn't use anything else with our dogs. Includes 66-page instruction booklet. Specify color: red, dark blue, light blue, black, tan and purple.

Complete Gentle Leader® Headcollar system $35.50

Contains headcollar, matching leash, indoor drag line and 66-page instruction booklet.

Snappy Trainer™ Training Device for dogs and cats $9.95

A mousetrap like device that makes a noise and jumps in the air when disturbed. Startles, but doesn't harm the offending animal. Safe. Won't trap noses, paws or children's fingers. Helps to stop undesirable behavior such as getting in the trash, stealing food, jumping on furniture and counters. Has kept our dogs Ashley and Mocha and our cat Buffett out of the trash for years! Comes three to a pack.

SSSCAT Automated Repellent $49.99

A battery operated device that senses the presence of a cat or dog and then makes an audible warning sound and sprays a jet of harmless mist. The sound and spray will startle the animal and cause her to move away. Great for keeping cats and dogs off counters, furniture, plants or specific areas of the house. Works on other small animals like rabbits and ferrets. For indoor use only, works on 4 AAA batteries (not included). Spray refills are available.

This is a wonderful way to deter animals from going where you don't want them, like kitchen counters or closets. This has worked well to keep our cat Buffett off the kitchen counter!

Anti-Icky-Poo® Enzymatic Cleaner $15.95 - 1 quart
                                                        $29.95 - 1 gallon
Large Syringe (To inject AIP into carpets/fabrics) $7.00

Works by biological action to remove odors safely and completely. Works on odors from urine, feces, vomit or other biological sources. Works on carpeting, rugs, furniture and any surface that can be cleaned with water. Fine fabrics should be tested for colorfastness before using.

The best product we've ever seen for removing dog and cat elimination odors! We couldn't live without it!

ORDER FORM

Listed below are the products mentioned in this book, and other products you might find useful. These products and more can be purchased through our secure shopping cart at
www.AnimalBehaviorAssociates.com
You may also order by phone at **303.932.9095** (phone) or by faxing this completed order form to **303.932.2298** (fax) or by mailing this form to **4994 S. Independence Way, Littleton, CO 80123**

Product	Price	Quantity	Total
"Canine Body Postures" Videotape	$ 49.95		
"What Dogs Need and How They Think"	5.00		
"76 Ways to Get Your Dog To Do What You Want"	5.00		
"Help! I'm Barking and I Can't be Quiet"	19.95		
"Raising a Behaviorally Healthy Puppy"	15.95		
Managing Chaos at the Door Specify: Audio CD or CD ROM	11.95		
Gentle Leader© Headcollar (collar and instruction book only) Specify: red, dark blue, light blue, black, tan, purple	25.50		
Gentle Leader© Headcollar - Complete System Specify: red, dark blue, light blue, black, tan, purple	35.50		
Snappy Trainer™ Training Device (3 pack)	9.95		
SSSCAT Automated Repellent	49.99		
Anti-Icky-Poo® Enzymatic Cleaner - 1 quart	15.95		
Anti-Icky-Poo® Enzymatic Cleaner - 1 gallon	29.95		
Large Syringe (to inject AIP into carpets/fabrics)	7.00		
		Subtotal	$
	Colorado residents **only** add 3.5% sales tax		
Shipping and handling charges: Orders up to $19.00 = $3.00 Orders from $19.01 to $150.00 = $7.00 Orders over $150.01 = $10.00			$
		GRAND TOTAL	$

Credit Card: ❑ [MasterCard] ❑ [VISA]

Name as it appears on card:_____

Credit card number:_____

Expiration date: _____ / _____

Your signature:_____

❑ Check enclosed. Make payable to **Animal Behavior Associates, Inc.**

Ship to: Name_____

          Address_____

          City/St/Zip_____